# MICROWAVE
## C·O·O·K·I·N·G

**GOLDEN APPLE PUBLISHERS**

MICROWAVE COOKING

A GOLDEN APPLE PUBLICATION/
PUBLISHED BY ARRANGEMENT WITH OTTENHEIMER PUBLISHERS INC.

JUNE 1986

GOLDEN APPLE IS A TRADEMARK OF GOLDEN APPLE PUBLISHERS

ISBN 0-553-19858-0

# Contents

# Appetizers

## Chicken Terrine

| | |
|---|---|
| 1 | **(3-pound) cooked chicken** |
| 1 | **pound raw pork sausage meat** |
| ½ | **pound sliced boiled ham, diced** |
| 2 | **cloves garlic, finely chopped** |
| 2 | **eggs, lightly beaten** |

| | |
|---|---|
| 1 | **teaspoon tarragon** |
| 1 | **tablespoon parsley, finely chopped** |
| ¼ | **cup brandy** |
| ½ | **teaspoon salt** |
| | **Freshly ground black pepper** |
| ½ | **cup butter, softened** |
| ½ | **pound sliced bacon** |

Discard the skin and bone and cut chicken into small pieces. Put chicken aside. Stir together all remaining ingredients except bacon.

Line a glass or ceramic casserole with half the bacon slices. Cover with 1/3 of the sausage mixture; top with 1/2 of the chicken. Continue forming layers; top with sausage mixture, and cover with remaining bacon.

Microwave on roast setting for 25 minutes. Rotate dish 1/4 of a turn after 15 minutes. Cool the terrine. Place it in refrigerator and weight it with 3 (1-pound) cans of food so it can be sliced without crumbling. Chill 12 hours before serving. Makes 8 servings.

## Escargots

| | |
|---|---|
| ½ cup butter | 2 dozen canned snails with |
| Dash of white pepper | shells |
| ½ teaspoon garlic powder | |
| ¼ cup fresh parsley, finely chopped | |

Place butter in small glass mixing bowl. Microwave on low 30 to 45 seconds to soften. Beat until fluffy. Add pepper, garlic powder, and parsley to butter; mix well.

Drain snails. Stuff each snail down into a shell. Fill each shell with 1-1/2 teaspoons parsley butter. Place on glass baking dish with shells upright. Microwave on low 3 to 4 minutes or until butter begins to bubble. Makes 4 servings.

**Note:** These appetizers may be made ahead and refrigerated. Increase cooking time by 30 seconds to 1 minute.

## Swiss Fondue

| | |
|---|---|
| 1 cup white wine (Chablis or California white wine) | Freshly ground black pepper |
| | 3 tablespoons kirsch |
| 2 whole cloves garlic, peeled | 3 tablespoons butter |
| ¾ pound (3 cups) Gruyère or Swiss cheese, grated | ¼ cup heavy cream |
| | 1 teaspoon salt |
| 3 tablespoons flour | |

Pour wine into a 1-1/2-quart earthenware pot, clay pot, or glass casserole. Add garlic. Microwave uncovered on low for 5 minutes. Discard garlic cloves.

Combine cheese, flour, and pepper and stir into hot wine. Microwave on low for 3 minutes. Stir in kirsch, butter, and cream. Cook on low for 4 more minutes. Season with salt.

Serve immediately with cubes of fresh, crusty French bread and chilled white wine. Spear bread cubes with fondue forks and swirl them into the hot fondue.

Mushroom caps, quickly fried in hot butter, as well as salami, carrot sticks, and cauliflower sprigs, make delicious contrasts of taste and texture with the fondue. In Switzerland there is also a bowl of pickled onions and potatoes boiled in their jackets to eat with the fondue. Makes 8 servings.

*Escargots*

## Meatball Appetizers

| | |
|---|---|
| 1 egg | ¼ cup fine fresh bread crumbs |
| 1 teaspoon soy sauce | |
| Freshly ground black pepper | ½ small onion, finely chopped |
| ½ teaspoon thyme | |
| 1 tablespoon oil | 1 tablespoon meat sauce such as A-1 |
| 1 pound ground lean chuck steak | |
| | ¼ cup milk |

Place all ingredients except oil in a bowl and stir lightly with a fork until just combined. Do not overmix or meatballs will become heavy. Form mixture into 1-inch balls.

Heat a ceramic plate on high for 4 minutes. Add oil. Cook 10 meatballs at a time for 1 minute on each side. Rotate dish 1/4 of a turn after the first minute. Makes 30, 1-inch meatballs.

## Stuffed Grape Leaves

| | |
|---|---|
| 1 (16-ounce) jar vine leaves | ½ teaspoon salt |
| 1½ tablespoons olive oil | Freshly ground pepper |
| 1 medium onion, finely chopped | ½ teaspoon cinnamon |
| ¾ cup rice | 2 medium-sized tomatoes, peeled, seeded, and chopped |
| 1½ cups water | |
| ½ cup white raisins, soaked in ½ cup water | Water |
| ½ cup pine nuts | Juice of 1 lemon |
| 2 tablespoons parsley, finely chopped | |

Unfold leaves carefully; rinse under cold water. Drain.

Heat oil in 1-quart glass or ceramic casserole on highest setting 30 seconds. Add onion; cook 1 minute. Add rice; cook 2 minutes. Stir in 1-1/2 cups water, drained raisins, and pine nuts. Cover; cook 10 minutes. Remove; let stand 10 minutes. Stir in parsley, seasonings, and tomatoes.

Place about 1 tablespoon mixture on each leaf. Fold stem end to enclose stuffing. Fold sides to center; roll to form neat package. (Do not fasten with toothpicks; rolls tear easily.) Place layer of leaves in glass baking dish; cover with layer of unfilled leaves, then with second layer of stuffed leaves. Add just enough water to cover leaves; add lemon juice. Weight with a plate. Cover with waxed paper and cook 20 minutes on highest setting. Allow to cool 1 hour. Drain; chill until serving time. Makes 6 servings.

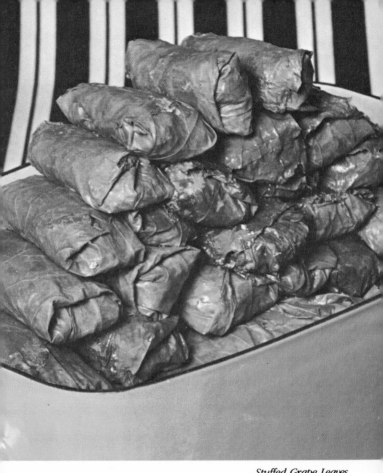

*Stuffed Grape Leaves*

## Creamed Mushrooms on Toast

| | |
|---|---|
| ¼ cup white wine | ¼ teaspoon pepper |
| 1 cup beef broth | ¾ cup butter |
| ¾ cup milk | 1 pound fresh mushrooms |
| ¼ cup all-purpose flour | ¼ cup chopped chives |
| ½ teaspoon salt | 12 slices bread |

Combine wine, beef broth, milk, flour, salt, and pepper in tall quart glass container. Microwave on high 2 minutes. Remove from oven; beat with wire whip or beater. Repeat cooking process 3 more times or until mixture thickens. Reserve.

Microwave 1/4 cup butter on high 2 minutes or until melted. Clean and slice mushrooms into "T" shapes. Add mushrooms and chives to butter. Cover; microwave on high 3 minutes, stirring once during cooking process. Add to cream sauce; stir to blend.

Toast bread slices; cut star shapes out of centers. Microwave 1/2 cup butter on low 30 seconds to soften. Spread on 6 toast stars; top with remaining toast slices. Serve mushrooms over toast sandwiches. Makes 3 servings.

## Liver Pâté

| | |
|---|---|
| ¼ cup butter | ¼ teaspoon pepper |
| 2 medium-sized onions, chopped | 1 cup fresh white bread crumbs |
| 1 pound chicken livers | 2 medium-sized eggs |
| 3 tablespoons dry sherry | 6 strips bacon |
| ¼ cup heavy table cream | Parsley for garnish |
| ½ teaspoon garlic salt | |

Heat butter in 1-quart glass baking dish on high for 20 seconds. Add onions and fry for 3 minutes. Add chicken livers, cover with a plate, and microwave on low for 8 to 10 minutes or until meat loses its pink color. Put livers and onions in a blender, add sherry and cream, and blend for 1 minute.

Season liver mixture with garlic salt and pepper. Stir in bread crumbs, then beat in eggs until mixture is smooth. Line a 1-1/2-pound glass loaf dish with bacon. Pour liver mixture into dish. Cover with plastic wrap. Microwave on low for 10 minutes. Cool pâté in pan, then unmold. Wrap in foil and store in refrigerator for up to 2 days to blend the flavors. Garnish with a sprig of parsley. Makes 6 or more servings.

## Pâté Maison

| | |
|---|---|
| ½ **pound ground raw pork** | 1 **teaspoon salt** |
| 1 **pound ground raw veal** | **Freshly ground black pepper** |
| 1 **pound ground raw calves** | 2 **tablespoons brandy** |
| **liver** | 2 **tablespoons Madeira** |
| 2 **cloves garlic, finely** | ½ **cup heavy cream** |
| **chopped** | 2 **eggs, lightly beaten** |
| ¾ **teaspoon thyme** | 4 **chicken livers, cut in half** |
| ¼ **teaspoon nutmeg** | 6 **slices bacon** |

Combine all ingredients except chicken livers and bacon in a large bowl. Do not stir too much or the mixture becomes heavy.

Place 1/2 of the mixture in a 9 × 5 × 2-1/2-inch glass loaf pan. Arrange chicken livers in a row down the length of the pan and cover with remaining mixture. Arrange bacon in overlapping slices on top of the pâté.

Microwave on roast setting for 25 minutes. Rotate pan 1/4 of a turn after 10 minutes.

Cool pâté. Cover with aluminum foil and weight the pâté with 3 (1-pound) cans of food so it can be sliced without crumbling. Chill for 48 hours before serving. Makes 10 servings.

## Savory Butter Scones

| | |
|---|---|
| 2 **cups self-rising flour** | 1 **small onion, finely** |
| 1 **teaspoon baking powder** | **chopped** |
| ½ **teaspoon salt** | 1 **clove garlic, crushed** |
| 2 **tablespoons butter** | 1 **teaspoon parsley, chopped** |
| ½ **cup cheese, grated** | ¼ **cup milk, approximately** |
| 1 **pimiento (canned)** | ⅓ **cup butter, melted** |

Sift dry ingredients into a bowl and cut in butter with 2 knives or pastry blender. Add cheese, chopped pimiento, onion, garlic, and parsley. Mix with enough milk to make a soft but not sticky dough.

Line bottom of an 8-inch glass baking dish with waxed paper. Pat out mixture in dish. Microwave on low for 7 minutes, and then on high for 3 to 4 minutes. Remove from oven and pour melted butter over the surface. Let stand for 5 minutes to set. Cut into fingers 1-1/2 × 3 inches and serve while hot. Makes about 15 scones.

*Goulash Soup*

## Garlic Shrimp

| | |
|---|---|
| 1½ **pounds shrimp, peeled and deveined** | 4 **tablespoons olive oil** |
| 4 **cloves garlic, peeled and left whole** | 1 **tablespoon lemon juice** |
| | ½ **teaspoon tarragon** |

Place shrimp in a shallow glass or ceramic baking dish with all remaining ingredients.

Microwave 8 minutes on high, until shrimp are pink. Turn shrimp and rotate dish 1/4 of a turn after 4 minutes. Serve hot, using toothpicks to pick up shrimp. Makes 4 servings.

## Marinated Steak Kebabs

| | |
|---|---|
| 1 **pound sirloin steak, weighed without the bone** | 1 **clove garlic, finely chopped** |
| ½ **cup red wine** | 2 **tablespoons cracked black pepper** |
| 2 **tablespoons oil** | |
| 1 **tablespoon soy sauce** | 2 **tablespoons oil** |

Cut steak into bite-sized cubes and place in a bowl. Add wine, 2 tablespoons oil, soy sauce, and garlic. Marinate steak for 2 hours. Remove and dry on paper towels. Press cracked pepper onto surface of the beef.

Heat microwave browning plate on high for 4 minutes. Add remaining 2 tablespoons oil. Add steak cubes and microwave for 2 minutes on each side. They should be rare in the center. Serve with toothpicks. Makes 6 servings.

**Note:** If your oven does not have a browning plate, use a shallow ceramic skillet.

## Satay Sauce

| | |
|---|---|
| 1 **medium-sized onion, peeled and finely chopped** | 1 **teaspoon sugar** |
| 1 **tablespoon oil** | ⅓ **cup peanut butter** |
| 1 **teaspoon garlic powder** | 1 **cup water** |
| ½ **teaspoon chili sauce** | 1 **tablespoon soy sauce** |
| | 1 **tablespoon lemon juice** |

Combine onion and oil in covered glass dish. Microwave on high 3 minutes, stirring once during cooking process. Add remaining ingredients. Microwave on high 6 minutes, stirring mixture twice during cooking process.

Serve sauce in a glass bowl for easy reheating. This is an excellent dipping sauce for beef cubes. Makes 1 cup.

# Soups and Salads

## Cream of Broccoli Soup

| | |
|---|---|
| 1½ pounds broccoli | 1 teaspoon salt |
| 1 onion, finely chopped | 3 cups chicken broth |
| 1 carrot, sliced | 1 cup light cream |
| 2 stalks celery with the leaves | ½ cup thinly sliced boiled ham, diced |
| 2 potatoes, peeled and chopped | ½ cup sour cream |

Discard lower third of the broccoli stems and chop remaining part into small pieces. Place in a 2-quart glass or ceramic casserole with onion, carrot, celery, potatoes, salt, and chicken broth. Cover and microwave on high for 10 minutes, until broccoli is tender.

Puree soup in a blender. Add cream and ham and microwave on high for 5 minutes, until very hot. Serve with a spoonful of sour cream. Makes 6 servings.

## Crab and Corn Soup

| | |
|---|---|
| 3 tablespoons butter | ½ teaspoon salt |
| ⅓ cup flour | ⅛ teaspoon pepper |
| 2 cups milk | ¼ cup table cream |
| 2 cups cold water | Slices of tomato (optional) |
| 1 (6-ounce) can crab meat | Watercress (optional) |
| 1 (12-ounce) can whole-kernel corn | |

Melt butter in a 1-1/2-quart glass or ceramic casserole for 30 seconds on high. Stir in flour with a wire whisk. While continuing to stir, gradually stir in milk and water. Cook for 5 minutes or until thickened. During cooking stir twice with whisk to make a smooth sauce.

Drain crab and corn. Break crab meat into pieces, removing cartilage. Stir crab meat and corn into the sauce. Season with salt and pepper. Cover casserole and microwave for 5 minutes on low. Remove from oven and stir in cream. Garnish with slices of tomato and watercress. Makes 4 servings.

## Goulash Soup

| | |
|---|---|
| 2 tablespoons butter | 4 cups stock (can be made with 4 bouillon cubes and 4 cups boiling water) |
| 2 tablespoons oil | |
| 3 medium-sized onions, sliced | Salt and pepper |
| 1 clove garlic, finely chopped | 2 medium-sized potatoes, sliced |
| 2 teaspoons paprika | 3 small tomatoes, chopped |
| ½ pound veal, ground | 6 thin slices French bread |
| ¼ pound pork, ground | |

Heat butter and oil in a 3-quart glass or ceramic casserole on high for microwave for 30 seconds. Stir in ground meats, and microwave for 2 minutes. Gradually add stock and season to taste. Cover and microwave on high for 5 minutes.

Add potato and tomato, and cook covered for 8 minutes longer, until potatoes are soft. Toast bread in toaster or in a broiler until crisp and brown. Serve with soup. Makes 6 servings.

Tomato Soup

## Tomato Soup

| | | | |
|---|---|---|---|
| 2 | pounds Italian plum tomatoes or about 6 medium-sized tomatoes | 1 | tablespoon tomato paste |
| 1 | onion, chopped | 1 | teaspoon basil or oregano |
| 1 | stalk celery, chopped | | Freshly ground black pepper |
| 2 | cups chicken broth | 1 | teaspoon salt |
| | | 1 | cup yogurt, or sour cream, or heavy cream (optional) |

Cut plum tomatoes in half or cut larger tomatoes into wedges to release juice. Place in a 3-quart glass or ceramic casserole with onion and celery. Add chicken broth, tomato paste, and basil or oregano and season with black pepper.

Microwave uncovered on high for 20 minutes. Season with salt. Strain to remove tomato skins and seeds. Garnish with spoonfuls of yogurt or sour cream or stir in whipping cream. Makes 6 servings.

## Scottish Hot Pot

| | | | |
|---|---|---|---|
| 2 | pounds lamb shoulder | 1 | scallion, white and green parts, thinly sliced |
| 6 | cups beef bouillon | 1 | small cauliflower, divided into florets |
| 1 | teaspoon salt | | |
| ½ | teaspoon pepper | 1 | (10-ounce) package frozen peas |
| 2 | onions, sliced | | |
| 2 | tablespoons butter | ½ | cup sherry |
| 2 | teaspoons flour | 2 | tablespoons parsley, finely chopped |
| 1 | stalk celery, diced | | |
| 2 | carrots, diced | | |
| 1 | turnip, diced | | |

In a 3-quart glass or ceramic casserole, place meat, bouillon, salt, pepper, and onions. Microwave on low for 30 minutes. Remove from oven. Cut meat into serving pieces.

Heat 2 tablespoons butter in a 1-quart glass bowl on high for 20 seconds. Brown meat in butter for 3 minutes and sprinkle with flour. Return meat to the stock and add celery, carrots, turnip, and scallion. Continue cooking for 15 minutes. Add cauliflower and peas to soup and cook for 8 minutes. Before serving, correct seasoning and sprinkle with parsley. Makes 6 servings.

## Chicken Soup

| | | | |
|---|---|---|---|
| 1 | (2½-pound) chicken, cut into serving pieces | 3 | chicken bouillon cubes |
| 4 | cups water | 1 | cup fresh peas |
| 1 | onion or 2 leeks, chopped | 2 | tablespoons parsley, chopped |
| 2 | carrots, diced | | Salt and pepper |

Place chicken in a 2-quart glass or ceramic casserole. Add 2 cups of water, onion or leeks, and carrots. Cover and microwave on high for 30 minutes.

Cool chicken and discard skin and bones. Cut meat into small pieces and place to one side. Skim fat from surface of the broth in the casserole. Add remaining 2 cups of water, bouillon cubes, peas, and parsley. Microwave for 2 minutes. Add chicken pieces and season with salt and pepper. Continue cooking, uncovered, for 2 more minutes, until soup is hot. Makes 4 servings.

## Vichyssoise

| | | | |
|---|---|---|---|
| 2 | pounds potatoes (about 4 medium-sized potatoes) | 1 | cup heavy cream |
| 6 | leeks or 3 yellow onions, finely chopped | 1 | teaspoon salt |
| 6 | cups chicken broth, hot | | Chopped chives |
| | | | Freshly ground black pepper |

Peel potatoes, cut into small pieces, and place in a 2-quart glass or ceramic casserole. Slice white part and lower third of the green part of the leeks. Wash in plenty of cold water to remove sand from the leeks. Add leeks or onions to potatoes along with the hot chicken broth. Cover and microwave on high for 10 minutes, until potatoes are very soft.

Puree soup in a blender. Add cream and salt and chill for 4 hours before serving. Garnish with chopped chives and black pepper. Makes 6 servings.

**Note:** Cold soups need more salt than hot soups.

## Apricot Dream Salad

| | | | |
|---|---|---|---|
| 1 | (8-ounce) package dried apricots | 2 | envelopes unflavored gelatin |
| 1½ | cups water | 1 | cup whipping cream* |
| ¼ | cup sugar | 3 | ounces cream cheese |
| 1 | tablespoon lemon juice | 2 | tablespoons rum |
| 1 | cup half-and-half | 16 | canned apricot halves |

Combine dried apricots, 1-1/4 cups water, and sugar in covered 1-1/2-quart glass casserole. Cover; microwave on high 10 minutes. Remove from oven; allow to stand 30 minutes to absorb liquid. Mix apricots and lemon juice in blender or puree until smooth. Cool; stir in half-and-half.

Soften gelatin in 1/4 cup water. Microwave on high 1 minute to dissolve gelatin. Stir gelatin into apricot mixture; mix thoroughly.

Whip cream with electric mixer until stiff; fold into apricot mixture. Oil a 1-1/2-quart mold. Pour in apricot mixture. Chill until set.

Heat cream cheese on low 30 to 45 seconds to soften. Add rum; whip until smooth. Fill 8 apricot halves with cream-cheese mixture; top with remaining apricot halves. Unmold salad on serving plate; garnish with stuffed apricots. Makes 8 servings.

\* For a tart taste, use 1 cup sour cream in place of whipping cream.

## Tomato Seafood Bowls

| | | | |
|---|---|---|---|
| ¼ | cup butter | 1 | cup cooked king crab meat, coarsely chopped |
| ¼ | cup green pepper, chopped | 1 | cup lobster meat, coarsely chopped |
| ¼ | cup onions, chopped | 6 | medium tomatoes |
| 2 | teaspoons seafood seasoning | 2 | tablespoons sherry |
| 1 | cup salad shrimp, steamed and cleaned | | Parsley sprigs |

Place butter in large glass casserole; microwave on medium 30 seconds to melt butter. Add pepper and onions; cover casserole. Microwave on high 5 minutes or until vegetables are soft but not mushy. Add seasonings; blend. Add seafood; microwave on high about 6 minutes or until heated thoroughly. Stir once during cooking process, stirring from outside toward inside of bowl to ensure even cooking.

Slice tops from tomatoes; remove pulp. Fill each tomato cup with fish mixture; pour 1 teaspoon sherry over fish in each tomato cup. Place tomatoes in glass baking dish; microwave on medium 4 to 5 minutes to heat tomato shells. *Do not overcook* or tomato shells will rupture.

Garnish tomatoes with parsley. Makes 6 servings.

# Main Courses

## German Sauerbraten

| | |
|---|---|
| 3 | **pounds boneless lean pot roast** |
| 1 | **medium onion, thinly sliced** |
| 1 | **tablespoon whole mixed pickling spices** |
| 1 | **cup wine vinegar** |
| 1 | **cup water** |
| ¼ | **teaspoon garlic powder** |
| 2 | **tablespoons vegetable oil** |
| 3 | **tablespoons all-purpose flour** |
| 3 | **tablespoons cold water** |
| ½ | **cup canned evaporated milk** |

Place meat and onion in glass bowl. Tie spices in small cloth bag; place in dish with meat and onions. Combine vinegar, 1 cup water, and garlic powder; pour over meat. Cover; refrigerate for 2 days. Turn meat twice a day. Remove meat and spices from marinade. Discard spices.

Preheat browning dish, uncovered, on high 7 minutes. Add 1 tablespoon oil. Place roast on dish; cook, uncovered, on high 2 minutes. Remove roast from dish; reheat dish on high 2 minutes. Add 1 tablespoon oil to preheated dish; brown other side of roast on high 3 minutes. Add marinade and onions to meat; cook on medium 30 minutes. Turn meat; cook 30 minutes on medium. Let stand, covered, 30 minutes to finish cooking. Remove meat from marinade.

Combine flour and 3 tablespoons cold water to form a paste; add to marinade. Return dish to oven; cook on high 2 minutes. Stir. Add milk; cook on high 1 to 2 minutes or until gravy thickens. Makes 6 servings.

*Sirloin Steaks with Flavored Butter*

## Corned Beef Hash

| | | | |
|---|---|---|---|
| 1 | pound corned beef, ground or finely chopped | 1 | onion, finely chopped |
| 2 | cups finely chopped cabbage (use a meat grinder or food processor if you have one), parboiled for 6 minutes | 2 | boiled potatoes, diced |
| | | ¼ | cup tomato puree |
| | | ½ | teaspoon salt |
| | | | Freshly ground black pepper |
| | | 2 | tablespoons oil |
| | | 2 | eggs, fried (optional) |

Combine all ingredients except the oil. Pour oil into a shallow 9-inch glass baking dish and microwave for 30 seconds on high. Add hash ingredients and cook 2 minutes. Stir hash and cook 3 minutes. Top with fried eggs if you wish. Makes 4 servings.

## Rolled Rib Roast

| | |
|---|---|
| 1 **(4-pound) boneless rolled rib roast** | **Salt and pepper** |

Place roast, fat side down, on a microwave oven roasting rack or on an inverted saucer in a glass or ceramic baking dish, to permit fat to drain. If roast rests directly on the baking dish, the under part will fry and then stew in its own juices.

Microwave on high for 12 minutes. Turn beef over and rotate the dish 1/4 of a turn and cook for another 12 minutes on roast setting. The internal temperature will read 118° to 120°F but will increase as much as 20 degrees as it stands. Season beef with salt and pepper and cover with aluminum foil. Let beef rest for 15 minutes before carving. This resting period is important, because if the beef is carved too quickly, it will be insufficiently cooked and the juices will pour out, leaving the meat dry and tasteless. Makes 8 servings.

## Pot Roast

| | |
|---|---|
| 1 **(3-pound) boneless chuck steak, in one piece, or cross-cut shoulder of beef** | 1 **bay leaf** |
| | 1 **teaspoon thyme** |
| | 3 **sprigs parsley** |
| | 10 **peppercorns** |

| *Marinade* | *Sauce* |
|---|---|
| 1½ **cups young red wine such as Beaujolais or California Mountain red wine** | 2 **tablespoons butter** |
| | 2 **tablespoons flour** |
| 2 **tablespoons oil** | 1¼ **cups cooking liquid from the casserole** |
| 1 **onion, chopped** | ½ **cup tomato sauce** |
| 1 **clove garlic, chopped** | ¼ **cup mayonnaise** |
| 1 **stalk celery, chopped** | ¼ **teaspoon thyme** |
| 1 **teaspoon salt** | |

Tie the beef at 1/2-inch intervals so it will keep its shape. Combine marinade ingredients in a 2-1/2-quart glass casserole. Place beef in the marinade. There should be enough liquid to cover the beef. If not, it will be necessary to turn the beef from time to time. Cover and refrigerate beef for 12 hours or up to 3 days.

Place beef, immersed in the marinade and covered, in the microwave oven. Microwave on low for 45 minutes. Turn beef over. Rotate the dish 1/4 of a turn after each 20 minutes. Allow to stand for 20 minutes before slicing.

Make sauce. Heat butter in a 4-cup glass measuring cup for 30 seconds on high. Stir in flour and cook for 20 seconds. Stir in all remaining sauce ingredients with a wire whisk. Microwave on low for 5 minutes. Serve with pot roast. Makes 6 servings.

*Deluxe Hamburgers*

## Beef Stewed in Red Wine

1½ pounds boneless chuck steak, cut into 1½-inch cubes
2 tablespoons butter
1 tablespoon oil
1 large turnip, cut into 1-inch pieces
1 rutabaga, cut into 1-inch pieces
1 pound small white onions, peeled
1 pound carrots, cut into 1-inch pieces
3 tablespoons flour
1 cup beef bouillon
1 cup red wine
Dash Worcestershire sauce
½ teaspoon peppercorns
3 bay leaves

Heat butter and oil in a 3-quart glass or ceramic casserole for 20 seconds. Brown beef, turnip, rutabaga, onions, and carrots for 4 minutes. Add flour, stir, and cook for another 2 minutes. Add bouillon, wine, Worcestershire sauce, peppercorns, and bay leaves. Cover and microwave on low for 50 minutes. Leave overnight and reheat next day. Makes 6 servings.

## Sirloin Steaks with Flavored Butter

2   **New York strip steaks,
    ¾ inch thick and
    approximately 8 ounces
    each**
1   **tablespoon butter or
    margarine**

*Chive Butter*
1   **stick unsalted butter**
¼   **cup chives, finely chopped**
**Salt and pepper to taste**

Wipe meat with damp cloth to remove excess blood and juices from surface.

Place browning dish in center of microwave oven; heat on high 5 minutes. Place butter in browning dish; tilt to coat. Add steaks; microwave on high 2 minutes. Remove steaks. Reheat browning dish on high 1 minute. Add steaks, uncooked-side-down; microwave on high 1-1/2 to 2 minutes more. Top with walnut-sized piece of chive butter (see below). Cover; allow to stand 5 minutes. Makes 2 servings.

**To make chive butter,** open wrapper on butter. Microwave on high 10 seconds; let stand 30 seconds. Continue in this manner until butter can be beaten easily with mixer. Beat butter, chives, salt, and pepper together until creamy. Place in container and refrigerate, or form into 1-inch-wide strip on piece of plastic wrap. Roll to enclose in wrap; slice off pieces as needed. Can be kept refrigerated several weeks.

## Beef Stew

2½ **pounds boneless chuck
    steak**
3   **tablespoons oil**
1   **onion, finely chopped**
1   **clove garlic, finely
    chopped**
2   **carrots, diced**

2   **stalks celery, sliced**
2   **tablespoons flour**
1½  **cups beef broth**
2   **teaspoons tomato paste**
½   **teaspoon thyme**
1   **bay leaf**

Trim beef and cut into 1-inch cubes. Brown cubes in hot oil on top of the stove or on your microwave browning plate; transfer to a 2-quart glass or ceramic casserole. Cook onion, garlic, carrots, and celery in the same oil for 2 minutes. Stir in flour and 1/2 cup of beef broth. Transfer to the casserole with the beef and add remaining broth and seasonings. Cover and microwave on low for 50 minutes.

Cool and chill overnight; then reheat on reheat speed for 10 minutes. Rotate dish and stir once after 5 minutes. Discard bay leaf before serving. Makes 6 servings.

*Teriyaki Meatballs*

## Chili

½  pound ground beef
1  tablespoon oil
½  small onion, finely chopped
1  clove garlic, finely chopped
2  teaspoons chili powder
¼  teaspoon ground cumin

Dash cayenne pepper
Dash Tabasco sauce
½  cup tomato sauce
2  cups canned tomatoes
½  teaspoon salt
1  (8-ounce) can red kidney beans, drained

Place ground beef in a 1-quart glass bowl. Microwave for 2 minutes on high and drain any accumulated fat. Fluff beef with a fork and put to one side. Heat oil in a custard cup for 20 seconds on the same setting.

Add onion and garlic and cook for 1 minute. Add chili and cumin and cook for 50 seconds. Stir these and all remaining ingredients except the beans into bowl with the ground beef. Cover and cook for 4 minutes. Stir in kidney beans and cook another 2 minutes. Makes 2 servings.

## Ground Beef and Noodles

| | |
|---|---|
| 1 pound ground chuck steak | ¾ cup sour cream |
| 1 tablespoon oil | 1 tablespoon tomato paste |
| 1 onion, finely chopped | 2 tomatoes peeled, seeded, and chopped |
| 1 clove garlic, finely chopped | 1½ cups cooked noodles or macaroni |
| 1 green pepper, finely chopped | ½ teaspoon salt |
| ½ teaspoon oregano | Freshly ground black pepper |
| ¼ cup beef broth | |

Preheat microwave browning dish on high for 4 minutes. Add beef and oil and cook for 2 minutes. Drain off any accumulated fat and transfer to a 2-quart glass or ceramic casserole. Add onion, garlic, and green pepper to casserole and cook for 2 minutes.

Add all remaining ingredients. Cover and cook for 5 minutes. Stir mixture once and rotate dish 1/4 of a turn after 3 minutes. Taste beef and season with salt and pepper. Makes 4 servings.

## Deluxe Hamburgers

| | |
|---|---|
| 1 pound ground chuck | 3 green onions, finely chopped |
| 1 medium-sized onion, finely chopped | ¼ cup Cheddar cheese, grated |
| 1 teaspoon salt | 2 tablespoons sour cream |
| ¼ teaspoon pepper | 4 hamburger buns |
| ½ teaspoon dry mustard | 8 cherry tomatoes, halved |
| 1 tablespoon chili sauce | 8 (1-inch) strips American cheese |
| 2 teaspoons Worcestershire sauce | |

Combine ground chuck, 1 onion, salt, pepper, dry mustard, chili sauce, and Worcestershire sauce; mix well. Form into 8 even-size hamburger patties.

Combine 3 green onions, Cheddar cheese, and sour cream; mix well. Spread this filling evenly over 4 hamburger patties. Top with remaining patties; seal edges.

Preheat microwave browning dish 6 minutes on high. Place hamburgers in dish; cook on high 5 minutes. Remove hamburgers; pour out grease. Return browning dish to oven; reheat on high 4 minutes. Place hamburgers in dish, being sure sides that faced inside the first time are now facing outside. Microwave on high 4 minutes. Cover; allow to rest 5 minutes.

*Macaroni-Cauliflower Casserole*

Check for doneness. (This length of cooking time produces medium hamburgers.)

    Place hamburgers on buns. Garnish each half with 4 tomato halves and 2 strips American cheese. Microwave on high 30 seconds or until cheese strips start to melt. Makes 4 servings.

## English Layered-Beef Pudding

| | |
|---|---|
| 1 | **pound basic bread dough (may be purchased in frozen form)** |
| 1 | **pound ground beef** |
| 4 | **strips bacon, cut into small pieces** |
| 2 | **small onions, chopped** |
| 1 | **clove garlic, finely chopped** |
| 1 | **teaspoon salt** |
| ½ | **teaspoon pepper** |
| 2 | **tomatoes** |
| ½ | **cup Cheddar cheese, grated** |
| 2 | **tablespoons whipping cream** |

Divide dough into 6 parts and roll out each section to fit size of casserole. Combine ground beef, onion, garlic, and seasonings, and arrange between layers of dough in an oiled 2-quart glass or ceramic casserole. Top with sliced tomato, grated cheese, and cream. Cover and microwave for 8 minutes on high. Turn dish 1/4 of a turn every 2 minutes. Leave pudding in the pan for 5 minutes. Makes 6 servings.

## Teriyaki Meatballs

**Meatballs**

| | |
|---|---|
| 1 | **pound lean ground beef** |
| 1 | **egg** |
| 1 | **slice bread, ground to crumbs** |
| ½ | **teaspoon salt** |
| 2 | **green onions, chopped** |
| 3 | **tablespoons water chestnuts, chopped** |
| ¼ | **teaspoon ground ginger** |
| 2 | **tablespoons cooking oil** |

**Sauce**

| | |
|---|---|
| ¼ | **cup soy sauce** |
| ½ | **cup crushed pineapple** |
| 2 | **tablespoons dry sherry** |
| ¼ | **teaspoon ground ginger** |
| 1 | **tablespoon sugar** |
| 1 | **tablespoon cornstarch** |
| ⅓ | **cup cold water** |

Combine ingredients for meatballs, except oil, in large mixing bowl; blend well. Form into small meatballs 1 inch in diameter.

Preheat microwave browning dish on high 5 minutes. Add oil; tilt to coat. Add meatballs; microwave on high 4 minutes, turning meatballs after 2 minutes. Drain; return to browning dish.

Combine soy sauce, pineapple, sherry, ginger, and sugar; mix well. Microwave on high 1-1/2 to 2 minutes (boiling). Combine cornstarch and water; add to sauce. Microwave on high 1-1/2 minutes, stirring once. Pour sauce over meatballs. Cover; microwave on medium 5 to 8 minutes to heat through. Makes 4 servings.

## Macaroni-Cauliflower Casserole

| | |
|---|---|
| 4 tablespoons butter | 1 tablespoon oil |
| 1 small onion, finely chopped | 4 ounces elbow macaroni (about 1 cup) |
| ½ pound ground beef | 2 tablespoons flour |
| 3 tablespoons catsup | 1¼ cups milk |
| 2¼ cups water | 1 egg, lightly beaten |
| 1½ teaspoons salt | 1 cup Cheddar cheese, grated |
| ⅛ teaspoon pepper | |
| 1 small cauliflower, broken into florets | Parsley sprigs for garnish |

Heat 2 tablespoons of the butter in a 1-quart glass casserole on high for 20 seconds. Add onion and ground beef and fry for 2 minutes. Drain fat and add catsup, 1/4 cup water, 1/2 teaspoon salt, and pepper; cook on reheat setting for 5 minutes.

In a separate covered glass casserole, cook cauliflower in 1/2 cup water for 8 minutes. Rotate dish 1/4 of a turn halfway through cooking period. Remove cauliflower with a slotted spoon.

Bring 2 cups of water, 1 tablespoon cooking oil, and 1 teaspoon salt to a full boil in a 2-quart glass casserole on high. Stir in macaroni. Re-cover, and cook on defrost setting for 10 to 12 minutes. Drain well.

Melt remaining 2 tablespoons of butter in a glass dish on high for 20 seconds. Stir in flour with a wire whisk. Gradually stir in the milk. Cook for 3 minutes or until thick. Stir twice during cooking to give a smooth sauce. Season to taste. Remove from heat and stir in beaten egg and 1/2 cup of the cheese.

Mix macaroni and cauliflower with the prepared sauce. Oil a 3-quart glass casserole and add ground beef mixture. Top with macaroni and cauliflower in cheese sauce. Sprinkle with remaining grated cheese. Cook on reheat setting for 5 minutes or until hot. Place in a preheated conventional oven at 400°F for the last 10 minutes to brown the topping. Garnish with parsley. Makes 4 servings.

## Skillet Supper

| | | | |
|---|---|---|---|
| ½ | pound ground beef | 1 | small green pepper, chopped |
| 3 | tablespoons oil | ½ | teaspoon salt |
| 2 | onions, sliced | ¼ | teaspoon pepper |
| 1 | clove garlic, minced | 4 | ounces egg noodles, cooked, drained |
| 1 | small eggplant, cut into ½-inch cubes | 6 | eggs |
| 1 | (8-ounce) can tomato sauce | ¼ | teaspoon cayenne pepper |

Place ground beef in a 1-quart glass bowl. Cook for 2 minutes on high; drain accumulated fat. Stir beef with a fork and put to one side.

Heat oil in a 12-inch glass bowl for 20 seconds on the same setting. Add onions and garlic and cook for 1 minute. Add ground beef, eggplant, tomatoes, green pepper, salt, and pepper. Cover and cook for 4 minutes. Add cooked noodles and mix thoroughly.

With back of spoon make 6 hollows in meat mixture. Break an egg into each hollow. Cover tightly with a lid or plastic wrap. Cook eggs on roast setting for about 8 minutes or until eggs are cooked to desired doneness. Let stand, covered, for 2 minutes before serving. Makes 6 servings.

## Tagliatelle Bolognese

**Meat Sauce**

| | | | |
|---|---|---|---|
| 2 | tablespoons butter | 1 | bay leaf |
| 1 | onion, finely chopped | ½ | cup beef bouillon |
| 1 | carrot, diced | ½ | teaspoon salt |
| 1 | stalk celery, diced | ⅛ | teaspoon pepper |
| 1 | clove garlic (optional), finely chopped | 1 | teaspoon sugar |
| 2 | strips bacon, diced | ¾ | pound Tagliatelle or other pasta |
| ½ | pound ground beef | ⅓ | cup Parmesan cheese, grated |
| 1 | (8-ounce) can tomato sauce | | |

Heat butter in a 3-quart glass casserole on high for 20 seconds. Add vegetables and diced bacon. Cook for 2 minutes. Add ground beef and microwave on high for 7 minutes; drain. Stir in tomato sauce, bay leaf, bouillon, salt, pepper, and sugar. Cover with a glass lid and cook on reheat setting for 7 minutes. Taste and add more seasoning if necessary. Remove bay leaf.

In a 3-quart covered glass casserole, bring 6 cups of water, 1 tablespoon cooking oil, and 1 teaspoon salt to a full boil on high. Stir in pasta and re-cover. Cook on defrost setting for 14 minutes or until tender. Drain and rinse thoroughly. Turn into a hot serving dish, pour cooked meat sauce into the center, and sprinkle with Parmesan cheese. Makes 4 to 6 servings.

*Calves Liver with Madeira Wine Sauce*

## Beef-Stuffed Zucchini Boats

| | |
|---|---|
| 4 **medium zucchini squash** | ½ **teaspoon crumbled sweet basil** |
| ½ **cup water** | 1 **cup fresh bread crumbs** |
| 1 **pound lean ground beef** | 1 **tablespoon parsley, chopped** |
| 2 **cloves garlic, minced** | 1¾ **cups tomato sauce** |
| 1 **medium onion, peeled and chopped** | ¼ **cup Parmesan cheese, grated** |
| ½ **cup green pepper, chopped** | **Salt and pepper** |
| ½ **teaspoon crumbled oregano** | |

Slice zucchini in half lengthwise. Scoop out pulp, leaving 1/2-inch-thick shell. Coarsely chop pulp.

Pour water into 9-inch-square or 11 x 7-inch glass baking dish. Microwave on high 3 minutes or until water is boiling. Add squash shells; cover. Microwave on high 3 minutes, rearranging once during cooking. Drain well; set aside.

Place ground meat in 2-quart Pyrex mixing bowl. Cover with paper towel; microwave on high 2-1/2 minutes. Stir meat; break up with fork. Stir in garlic, onion, and green pepper. Re-cover; microwave on high 2-1/2 minutes. Drain hamburger mixture. Stir in zucchini pulp, oregano, sweet basil, bread crumbs, parsley, and 1/4 cup tomato sauce. Mix well. Stuff squash shells with mixture. Place side by side in glass baking dish. Top with remaining 1-1/2 cups tomato sauce; sprinkle with cheese. Cover with plastic wrap. Microwave on medium 15 to 18 minutes. Serve hot. Makes 4 servings.

## Calves Liver with Madeira Wine Sauce

| | |
|---|---|
| 4 **slices bacon** | ½ **teaspoon liquid gravy seasoning** |
| 1 **pound calves liver** | 2 **tablespoons Madeira wine** |
| 1 **tablespoon flour** | **Salt and pepper** |
| ¾ **cup hot beef broth** | |

Place bacon in 9-inch-square browning dish; microwave on high 3 to 3-1/2 minutes or until well browned, turning and rearranging once. Remove bacon immediately. Roll into curls; drain on paper towels.

Meanwhile, drain liver; pat dry on paper towels. Place in bacon drippings. Microwave on high 1-1/2 minutes. Turn; microwave on high 1 minute. Remove; keep warm.

Stir flour into drippings. Cook 30 seconds or until bubbly. Combine beef broth, gravy seasoning, Madeira, and salt and pepper to taste; add to flour mixture, stirring well. Microwave on high 3 minutes, stirring once

*Apricot-Glazed Lamb Chops*

each minute. Pour hot gravy over liver. Garnish with bacon curls and sautéed onions or baked bananas. Makes 4 servings.

**Baked Bananas:** Peel 4 firm bananas; cut in half crosswise. Brush with melted butter; roll in 3/4 cup soft bread crumbs. Place on rack; broil until lightly browned.

## Apricot-Glazed Lamb Chops

| | |
|---|---|
| 3 **tablespoons butter** | 2 **tablespoons cornstarch** |
| 1 **onion, chopped** | ½ **teaspoon ginger** |
| 6 **(3-ounce) lamb chops** | 1 **tablespoon lemon juice** |
| ¾ **cup apricot preserves** | |
| 2 **tablespoons Worcestershire sauce** | |

Melt butter in large glass baking dish on medium 1 minute. Add onion; cover. Cook on high 2 minutes. Add lamb chops to dish, being sure bones are turned toward middle. Cover; cook on high 4 minutes. Rearrange chops in dish, moving those in center to outside. Cover; microwave on high 4 minutes.

Remove chops from dish. Add remaining ingredients to butter and onions; stir to mix. Cover; microwave on high 2 minutes and 30 seconds. Stir to thicken. Return lamb chops to dish. Cover; microwave on high 4 minutes. Rearrange chops as before. Cover; cook on high 4 additional minutes or until chops are no longer pink. Let stand 5 minutes before serving. Makes 6 servings.

## Lamb Chops Braised in Red Wine

| | |
|---|---|
| 6 **thick loin lamb chops** | 1 **cup red wine** |
| 2 **tablespoons oil** | ½ **cup beef broth** |
| 1 **onion, finely chopped** | 1 **teaspoon basil** |
| 1 **clove garlic, finely chopped** | 1 **bay leaf** |
| 2 **tomatoes, chopped** | **Salt and pepper** |
| ½ **cup tomato puree** | 1 **tablespoon butter** |
| | 2 **tablespoons flour** |

Trim lamb chops. Heat microwave browning dish for 4 minutes on high. Add oil and cook the chops, 1 at a time, for 1 minute on each side. Transfer chops to a 2-quart glass or ceramic casserole and add all remaining ingredients except butter and flour. Cover and cook on roast setting for 30 minutes. Remove chops. Arrange them on a hot serving plate and keep them warm while preparing the sauce.

Strain liquid from the casserole. Heat butter on high for 30 seconds. Stir in flour and cook for 30 seconds. Stir in strained cooking liquid with a wire whisk. Taste, add salt and pepper, and reheat if necessary. Serve sauce over lamb chops or separately. Makes 6 servings.

*Roast Lamb*

## Lamb Rib Roast With Parsley Dressing

1   **rib lamb roast (preferably French cut)**
1   **bunch parsley, chopped**
1   **cup seasoned bread crumbs**
**Salt and pepper**

Slit the roast, forming a 3-inch-long pocket at top of roast (ribs pointing up). Fill with a mixture of seasoned bread crumbs and chopped parsley. Salt and pepper the roast.

Microwave on roast setting for 10 minutes, turning after 5 minutes. Then microwave for another 4 minutes on medium. Let set for 5 minutes after removing from oven. Makes 8 servings.

## Roast Lamb

| | | | |
|---|---|---|---|
| 1 | (5-pound) leg of lamb with the bone | 1 | teaspoon rosemary |
| 3 | cloves garlic | | Freshly ground pepper |
| 3 | tablespoons butter, melted | | Salt |

Trim excess fat from the lamb. Make a series of slits in the surface of the lamb with the point of a sharp knife. Cut garlic into slivers and insert tiny pieces of garlic into slits. Brush lamb with melted butter. Press rosemary onto surface of the lamb and season with pepper.

Place lamb fat-side-down on a rack or on an inverted saucer set in a glass or ceramic baking dish. Microwave on high for 20 minutes. Turn lamb on its other side and brush with butter. Cook on roast setting for 20 minutes longer (150°F) for rare lamb; 25 more minutes (160°F) for medium lamb; and 30 more minutes (170°F) for well-done lamb. (If your oven does not have a roast setting, place a glass of hot water in the oven during this stage of cooking to slow the cooking process). Season with salt and cover with aluminum foil. Allow to stand for 15 minutes before carving. The temperature will continue to rise during this resting time. Makes 6 servings.

**Note:** For rare lamb, cook 8 minutes per pound; for medium lamb, cook 9 minutes per pound; and for well-done lamb, cook 10 minutes per pound.

## Lamb Pilaf

| | | | |
|---|---|---|---|
| 2 | tablespoons oil | 1 | cup zucchini or other green vegetable, cooked and sliced |
| 1 | onion, finely chopped | | |
| ¼ | teaspoon allspice | ⅓ | cup slivered almonds |
| ¼ | teaspoon cinnamon | ⅓ | cup raisins, soaked in hot water for 5 minutes and drained |
| ¼ | teaspoon thyme | | |
| 2 | cups cooked lamb, cut into bite-sized pieces | | |
| 3 | cups cooked rice | ½ | cup beef broth |
| 1 | tomato, peeled, seeded, and chopped | | |

Heat oil in a 1-1/2-quart glass or ceramic casserole on high. Fry onion in the oil for 1 minute. Stir in spices and cook for 30 seconds. Stir in all remaining ingredients and cook for 8 minutes. Rotate the dish 1/4 of a turn every 2 minutes. Makes 6 servings.

*Lamb Stew*

## Butterfly Leg of Lamb

| | |
|---|---|
| 1 **(3-pound) leg of lamb, weighed after the bone is removed** | 1 **teaspoon rosemary** |
| | 3 **tablespoons butter** |
| **slice bread, broken into 6 pieces** | 2 **cloves garlic, finely chopped** |
| ½ **cup parsley** | **Salt and pepper** |

Ask the butcher to remove the bone from the lamb and "butterfly" it. Place lamb, fat-side-down, on a microwave oven roasting rack or on top of an inverted saucer set in a glass baking dish. Place bread, parsely, and rosemary in a blender and blend until finely chopped. Spread mixture on the surface of the lamb.

Heat butter and garlic in a custard cup on high for 40 seconds. Drizzle garlic butter over the lamb. Microwave lamb on high for 10 minutes. Rotate dish 1/4 of a turn and cook on roast setting for 8 minutes. Season with salt and pepper and leave to rest for 10 minutes before slicing. Makes 6 servings.

---

## Lamb Stew

| | |
|---|---|
| 1 **pound boneless lamb, cut into 6 pieces** | 2 **cups water** |
| | 1 **clove garlic, minced** |
| 1 **tablespoon flour** | ½ **pound carrots, cubed** |
| 2 **teaspoons salt** | 2 **turnips, cubed** |
| ¼ **teaspoon pepper** | ¼ **pound fresh green beans** |
| 3 **tablespoons oil** | ¼ **pound fresh green peas** |
| 1 **cup white wine** | 6 **small potatoes** |
| 1 **tablespoon tomato paste** | 1 **onion, diced** |

Combine flour, salt, and pepper. Coat lamb in seasoned flour. Place oil in a 2-quart glass casserole with meat. Cover and cook on roast setting for 10 minutes.

Add wine, tomato paste, water, and garlic and bring to boil on high. Add all vegetables except peas and cook covered on low for 35 minutes. Add peas and cook 4 minutes longer. Makes 4 servings.

*Sausage and Rice Casserole*

## Lamb Shanks

| | |
|---|---|
| 3 tablespoons oil | 1 onion, finely chopped |
| 4 lamb shanks, weighing approximately 12 ounces each | 2 cloves garlic, finely chopped |
| 3 tablespoons flour | 4 carrots, chopped into 1-inch pieces |
| 1½ cups beef broth | 1 (8½-ounce) package frozen peas |
| 1 teaspoon rosemary | |

Heat oil in a skillet and brown shanks on all sides. Transfer to a 2-1/2-quart glass or ceramic casserole. Stir flour into the oil. Add beef broth gradually, stirring to form a smooth sauce. Add all remaining ingredients, except peas, and pour over the lamb. Cover and cook on roast setting for 50 minutes.

Add peas and continue cooking for 10 minutes at the same setting. Makes 4 servings.

## Baked Ham with Mustard Crust

| | |
|---|---|
| 1 (5-pound) fully cooked ham | 2 egg yolks |
| 1 (8-ounce) jar apricot preserves | 1½ cups freshly made bread crumbs |
| 2 teaspoons dry English mustard powder | ¼ cup parsley |
| | ¼ cup chopped chives |
| 2 teaspoons Dijon mustard | 1 teaspoon marjoram |
| 1 tablespoon cornstarch | 3 tablespoons butter, melted |

Score ham fat in a diamond pattern after removing rind. Place ham, fat-side-down, in a microwave oven roasting rack or set on 2 saucers inverted in a glass baking dish. Cook on roast setting for 25 minutes. Remove the ham from the oven.

Remove lid from the apricot preserves and heat in the jar on high for 5 minutes. Force hot preserves through a strainer and brush the clear liquid over ham. Rotate dish 1/4 of a turn and continue cooking on roast setting for 20 minutes. Remove from oven and check temperature with a meat thermometer. The reading should be 150°F. The temperature will rise 10 degrees as it stands. Leave ham to rest for 15 minutes.

Preheat conventional oven to 375°F. Combine mustard powder, mustard, and cornstarch. Stir in egg yolks. Spread mixture over surface of the ham.

Place bread crumbs, parsley, chives, and marjoram in a blender and blend until herbs are finely chopped. Press bread crumbs lightly over the mustard covering. Place ham on a roasting rack. Drizzle with melted butter. Cook in the preheated oven for 20 minutes until crumbs are lightly browned. Makes 10 servings.

## Sugar-Baked Ham

| | |
|---|---|
| 1 (3-pound) boneless, ready-to-eat ham | 3 cups water |
| | 1 tablespoon corn oil |
| 2 bay leaves | ⅓ cup brown sugar |
| 6 peppercorns | Watercress for garnish |

Place ham in a large glass casserole. Add bay leaves and peppercorns. Bring to a boil on high. Reduce heat to low and cook for 20 minutes.

Remove from liquid and remove rind from ham. Brush ham with oil and sprinkle surface of ham with sugar. Cook on roast setting for 15 minutes. Cover and let stand for another 15 minutes before slicing. Garnish with watercress. Makes 6 servings.

*Veal Stroganoff with Noodles*

## Pork Roast with Prunes

| | |
|---|---|
| 12 large dried prunes | 1½ teaspoons salt |
| 1 cup beef bouillon | 2 large red apples |
| 4 pounds boneless pork | ¾ cup water |
|     roast, cut into 1-inch slices | 1 tablespoon sugar |
| ½ teaspoon pepper | ½ teaspoon lemon juice |
| ¼ teaspoon ground ginger | Parsley, for garnish |

Soak prunes in bouillon overnight. Remove and pit. Reserve bouillon and 4 prunes. Mix remaining prunes with pepper and ginger. Push them in between the slices of the roast. Place pork on a microwave oven roasting rack or on an inverted saucer in a glass baking dish to permit fat to drain. Microwave on high for 24 minutes. Turn pork over and rotate dish 1/4 of a turn and cook for another 20 to 24 minutes on roast setting. Remove from oven and transfer to serving platter. Sprinkle with salt and cover with aluminum foil. Let pork roast rest for 15 minutes before serving. The pork will continue cooking.

Pour off fat from roasting pan. Add reserved bouillon. Bring to boil on high for 2 minutes. Stir and continue cooking to reduce juices.

Core apples. Slice each into 4 rings. Put water and sugar in a 1-quart glass dish. Heat for 1 minute to dissolve sugar; add lemon juice. Place apple rings in liquid and microwave on high for 3 minutes or until apples are soft but not mushy. Place apple rings around pork and fill center of each ring with a prune. Garnish with parsley. Makes 4 servings.

## Pork with Rice and Oranges

| | |
|---|---|
| 2 cups roast pork, diced | ¼ cup raisins soaked for 5 |
| 2 tablespoons oil |     minutes in hot water and |
| 1 small onion, finely |     drained |
|     chopped | 2 cups chicken broth |
| 1 cup long-grain rice | ½ cup orange juice |
| 1 teaspoon paprika | 1 tablespoon butter |
| 1 teaspoon cinnamon | Salt and pepper |
| 1 teaspoon cumin | Grated rind of 2 oranges |
| ½ cup pine nuts or slivered | 2 oranges, sliced |
|     almonds | |

Trim pork of all fat. Heat oil in a 2-quart glass or ceramic casserole on high for 20 seconds. Add onion and cook for 1 minute. Add rice and cook for 1 minute. Stir once. Rotate dish 1/4 of a turn and cook 1 more minute.

Add all remaining ingredients except sliced oranges. Add pork. Cover and cook for 10 minutes. Let stand 10 minutes. Garnish with sliced oranges heated in the microwave oven for 1 minute. Makes 4 servings.

*Roast Chicken Royal*

## Look for additional AZO products for UTI detection, pain and support.

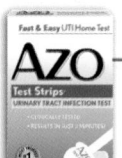

### AZO Test Strips®

- Fast and easy at-home UTI detection
- Clinically tested
- Results in just 2 minutes

### AZO Urinary Pain Relief™

- Relieves UTI pain, burning and urgency fast
- Targets the source of pain

### AZO Cranberry®

- Helps flush to maintain urinary tract cleanliness*

To learn more visit: **www.AZOProducts.com**

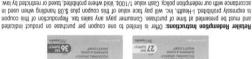

## Casserole of Pork and Apples

| | | | |
|---|---|---|---|
| 3 | pounds boneless pork loin, cut into 1½-inch cubes | 1 | teaspoon cumin powder or curry powder |
| 2 | tablespoons oil | 2 | tablespoons flour |
| 4 | leeks, washed and sliced, or 2 onions, sliced | 1¼ | cups apple cider |
| 2 | green cooking apples, peeled, cored, and sliced | ¼ | cup apple brandy or white vermouth |
| | | 1 | teaspoon salt |
| | | | Freshly ground black pepper |

Brown pork in hot oil in a skillet and transfer cubes to a casserole. Cook leeks or onions and apples in same oil for 3 minutes until softened. Stir in cumin or curry powder and cook 1 minute. Stir in flour and all remaining ingredients.

Transfer to a 2-quart glass or ceramic casserole. Cover and cook in microwave oven for 1 hour on roast setting. Rotate dish 1/4 of a turn after 30 minutes. Allow to rest 10 minutes before serving. Makes 6 servings.

## Chinese Spareribs with Sweet-and-Sour Sauce

| | | | |
|---|---|---|---|
| 3 | pounds spareribs | | *Sweet-and-Sour Sauce* |
| | Freshly ground black pepper | ½ | cup sugar |
| 1 | teaspoon sugar | ½ | cup vinegar |
| 1 | tablespoon soy sauce | 2 | tablespoons soy sauce |
| 2 | tablespoons dry sherry | 2 | tablespoons dry sherry |
| 2 | carrots, cut diagonally into 1-inch pieces | 3 | tablespoons tomato catsup |
| 1 | onion, cut into 1-inch chunks | 2 | tablespoons cornstarch, dissolved in ½ cup pineapple juice |
| 2 | green peppers, cut into 1-inch diamonds | | |
| 2 | tablespoons oil | | |
| 8 | mushroom caps | | |
| 1 | (8-ounce) can pineapple cubes, drained | | |

Place spareribs in a 12-inch glass or ceramic baking dish with the meatiest part to the edges. Add pepper, sugar, soy sauce, and sherry. Cover with waxed paper and cook on roast setting for 30 minutes. Remove from oven.

Place carrots, onion, and green peppers in a 1-quart glass or ceramic casserole. Cover with boiling water and microwave on high for 5 minutes. Drain the vegetables.

*Chicken Fricassee*

Heat ceramic browning dish on high for 4 minutes. Add oil. Brown drained vegetables for 3 minutes. Add mushroom caps and pineapple cubes; cook 2 minutes. Add barbecued ribs.

Combine all ingredients for the sweet-and-sour sauce in a 4-cup glass measuring cup and cook on high for 2 minutes. Stir and pour over spareribs. Heat 2 minutes, until very hot. Serve with rice. Makes 4 servings.

## Sausage and Rice Casserole

| | |
|---|---|
| 2 tablespoons butter or margarine | 1 (5-ounce) package yellow rice mix (chicken-flavored rice mix may be substituted) |
| ¼ cup onion, minced | |
| ¼ cup celery, minced | |
| 1 pound mild bulk pork sausage | 2 cups boiling water |
| | ¼ cup Parmesan cheese, grated |

Place butter in small bowl or casserole; microwave on high 40 seconds. Add onion and celery; stir. Microwave on high 2 minutes.

Place sausage in 2-1/2-quart casserole; break into chunks with fork. Microwave on high 5 minutes, stirring well after 2 1/2 minutes. Drain well. Add onion-and-celery mixture and rice mix to cooked sausage in casserole; stir well. Add boiling water. Cover tightly with plastic wrap; microwave on medium 15 to 20 minutes or until liquid is absorbed. Let stand 5 minutes.

Fluff rice with fork; sprinkle with Parmesan cheese. Serve hot with hard rolls and scrambled eggs. Makes 4 or 5 servings.

## Veal Stroganoff with Noodles

| | |
|---|---|
| 1 small onion | ¼ teaspoon pepper |
| 1 clove garlic | 1 cup sour cream |
| ¼ cup butter | |
| 1½ pounds 1-inch veal cubes | ***Noodles*** |
| 1 dozen fresh mushrooms | 3 cups hot tap water |
| 2 tablespoons tomato paste | 2 cups noodles |
| 1 teaspoon salt | |

Peel onion and garlic; chop fine. Combine butter, onion, and garlic in covered casserole dish. Microwave on high 4 minutes, stirring once during cooking process.

Stir in veal; cover. Microwave on high 8 minutes or until meat is no longer pink. Add mushrooms, tomato paste, salt, and pepper. Cover; cook on high 5 to 6 minutes or until mushrooms are tender. Stir in sour cream; cover. Microwave on medium 3 minutes or until thoroughly heated.

To make noodles, pour water into 3-quart covered casserole; microwave on high 6 minutes. Add noodles; continue cooking on high 6 minutes. Let noodles set 5 minutes before draining.

Serve stroganoff over noodles. Makes 4 servings.

**Note:** To prevent water from boiling over, set lid ajar during cooking process.

*Chicken Curry*

## Barbecued Chicken

| | | | |
|---|---|---|---|
| 1 | (3-pound) chicken, cut into serving pieces | 1 | teaspoon honey or sugar |
| | | 1 | teaspoon mustard |
| | | 1 | tablespoon meat sauce or Worcestershire sauce |
| **Barbecue Sauce** | | | |
| ½ | cup catsup | 1 | clove garlic, finely chopped |
| 2 | tablespoons chile sauce | | |

Place chicken in a 10-inch glass baking dish. Place breasts in the center of dish. Combine barbecue sauce ingredients and brush sauce over surface of the chicken. Cook, uncovered, on roast setting for 30 minutes.

Turn chicken pieces over after 15 minutes. Brush with remaining barbecue sauce; rotate dish 1/4 of a turn. Makes 4 servings.

## Roast Chicken Royal

2½ cups white bread crumbs
1¼ cups milk
1 large egg, beaten
2 medium-sized mushrooms, cleaned and chopped
¼ pound ground veal
¼ pound ground pork
½ teaspoon salt
¼ teaspoon pepper
1 (4½-pound) chicken
2 strips bacon, uncooked
1 clove garlic, minced or crushed
1 tablespoon cooking oil
2 cups chicken broth or bouillon
1 tablespoon cornstarch
1 small jar artichoke hearts
1 (8-ounce) can mushrooms, drained
1 bunch watercress
1 large orange, cut into wedges

Put bread crumbs and milk in a bowl. Cover and let stand for 30 minutes. Add beaten egg, chopped mushrooms, veal, and pork. Season well with salt and pepper. Mix to form a firm stuffing.

Dry chicken skin on paper towels. Season inside with salt and pepper. Put bacon and garlic inside chicken; stuff. Truss the chicken and place it breast-side-down on a microwave oven roasting rack or on an inverted saucer set in a glass baking dish. Brush skin with oil.

Cook for 16 minutes on high. Turn chicken breast-side-up and rotate pan 1/4 of a turn. Cook on roast setting for 16 more minutes, basting frequently with 1 tablespoon oil or drippings from the pan. Transfer chicken to a serving dish and let it rest for 15 minutes before carving.

Strain off all but 2 tablespoons of fat from roasting pan; add chicken stock. Stir cornstarch with 2 tablespoons of cold water; stir into juices in baking dish. Bring to boil on high and cook for 2 minutes or until thick. Stir once after 1 minute.

In separate glass bowls, heat mushrooms and artichoke hearts in juice from containers. Cook for 2 minutes or until warm. Drain. Garnish chicken with artichoke hearts, mushrooms, watercress, and orange wedges. Makes 4 servings.

## Chicken Fricassee

2 tablespoons butter
1 onion
3 stalks celery
2 egg yolks
1 (10½-ounce) can cream of chicken soup
¼ teaspoon marjoram
¼ teaspoon thyme
½ teaspoon salt

*Chicken Marengo*

Melt butter in covered shallow baking dish on medium 2 minutes. Finely chop onion and celery; add to melted butter. Cover; microwave on high 3 minutes. Stir.

Combine egg yolks and chicken soup; beat well. Stir mixture and seasonings into cooked vegetables. Cover; microwave on high 1 minute. Remove from oven; stir with whisk to distribute egg yolks evenly throughout sauce.

In separate dish, heat chicken on high 2 minutes. Add chicken to sauce. Cover; cook on high 3 minutes. Let stand, covered, 5 minutes before serving.

Serve fricassee on bed of rice garnished with black mushrooms. Makes 4 servings.

## Chicken Breasts with Lemon and White Vermouth

| | |
|---|---|
| 8 **boneless chicken breasts with skin removed** | **Salt and pepper** |
| 4 **tablespoons butter** | |
| 4 **scallions, finely chopped** | ***Sauce for the Chicken Breasts*** |
| **Grated rind and juice of 1 lemon** | ½ **cup whipping cream** |
| ½ **teaspoon tarragon or marjoram** | 1 **tablespoon cornstarch dissolved in 2 tablespoons cold water** |
| ⅓ **cup white vermouth** | 2 **tablespoons parsley, finely chopped** |

Arrange chicken breasts in a 10-inch glass baking dish. Dot with butter and add all remaining ingredients except salt and pepper. Cover chicken with waxed paper. Cook on roast setting for 15 minutes.

After 7 minutes rearrange chicken, placing center pieces at edge of dish. Rotate dish 1/4 of a turn. Season with salt and pepper immediately after chicken breasts are cooked.

Remove chicken from baking dish. Arrange on a bed of steaming hot rice and keep it hot while preparing the sauce.

Pour cream into baking dish and cook on high with the juices from the chicken breasts for 1 minute, until hot. Stir in cornstarch dissolved in cold water; heat for 1 minute. Stir with a wire whisk. Season with salt and pepper and pour sauce over chicken breasts. Garnish with parsley. Makes 4 servings.

## Chicken Curry

| | |
|---|---|
| 1 **(2½- to 3-pound) broiler-fryer chicken, cut up** | 1 **teaspoon curry powder** |
| ¼ **teaspoon ground ginger** | 1 **tablespoon peanut butter** |
| 1 **teaspoon seasoned salt** | **Chicken broth** |
| 3 **tablespoons flour** | ½ **cup coconut milk** |
| 2 **tablespoons olive oil** | ¼ **teaspoon ground cardamom** |
| 1 **medium onion, peeled and chopped** | ¼ **teaspoon ground cloves** |
| 2 **cloves garlic, peeled and minced** | ½ **teaspoon ground cinnamon** |
| | 2 **tablespoons lemon juice** |

Wash chicken; pat dry. Rub chicken with ginger and salt. Shake 1 tablespoon flour inside oven-roasting bag. Add chicken pieces; close bag with rubber band. Make several 1/2-inch slits in bag. Place in baking dish; cook on high 15 to 18 minutes or until chicken is cooked through. Let stand 10 minutes. Drain juices from bag; reserve. Remove chicken from bag and arrange in casserole dish. Set aside.

Place oil in 1-quart casserole. Add onion and garlic, stirring well. Microwave on high 2 minutes. Add curry powder, peanut butter, and 2 tablespoons flour; mix well. Microwave on high 1 minute.

*Spatchcock Turkey*

Add enough chicken broth to reserved juices to make 1-1/2 cups. Add chicken broth and coconut milk to flour mixture; stir well with wire whisk. Microwave on high 3 minutes, stirring once each minute. Add remaining ingredients; mix well. Pour sauce over chicken; cover. Microwave on high 3 to 4 minutes to heat through. Makes 4 servings.

## Stuffed Chicken Legs

| | |
|---|---|
| 4 ounces salami | 1 teaspoon salt |
| 1 large onion | 2 eggs |
| 2 tablespoons parsley | ¼ cup milk |
| 10 chicken legs | 2 cups dried bread crumbs, |
| 1 cup flour | crushed |
| ¼ teaspoon pepper | |

Chop salami, onion, and parsley very fine. Place in bowl; mix well. Gently loosen skin around chicken legs, starting at thick end of leg, being careful not to cut or tear skin. Carefully pack salami mixture evenly under skin of each leg.

Combine flour and seasonings; pour into shallow bowl. Beat eggs and milk together; pour into shallow bowl. Pour bread crumbs into shallow bowl.

Roll legs in seasoned flour. Coat with beaten eggs; cover with bread crumbs. Brown legs in oil heated to 360°F. Drain on paper towels. Arrange legs on microwave roasting rack with bone side to center and flesh end out. Microwave on high 10 minutes. Rearrange chicken on roasting rack by moving center legs to outside and moving outside legs to center. Return chicken to oven; microwave on high 5 minutes. Let stand 5 minutes; check for doneness by inserting microwave thermometer into fleshy part of a center leg. Approximate cooking time on high for 10 chicken legs is 15 to 20 minutes. Makes 5 servings.


## Chicken Marengo

| | |
|---|---|
| 1 (2½- to 3-pound) broiler-fryer chicken, cut up | ¼ teaspoon crumbled thyme |
| | 1 bay leaf |
| 3 tablespoons olive oil | Salt and pepper |
| 1 clove garlic, minced | ¼ pound mushrooms, sliced |
| 1 onion, thinly sliced | 1 cup cooked small shrimp |
| ½ cup chicken broth | Garlic croutons |
| ½ cup white wine | Poached eggs |
| 1 (6-ounce) can tomato paste | Chopped parsley |

Wash chicken. Remove skin; pat dry. Preheat browning dish on high 5 minutes. Add olive oil; tilt to coat. Add garlic and onion; microwave on high 1 minute. Remove from pan with slotted spoon; reserve. Add chicken parts; microwave on high 4 minutes. Turn; microwave on high 3 additional minutes.

In glass measuring cup, combine chicken broth, wine, tomato paste, thyme, bay leaf, salt, and pepper; mix well. Microwave on high 2-1/2 minutes or until boiling.

*Flounder Rolls with Shrimp Sauce*

Arrange onion and mushrooms over chicken. Pour sauce over all. Cover; microwave on high 16 to 18 minutes or until chicken is fork-tender. Stir in shrimp; heat for 1 minute. Arrange chicken on serving platter. Pour sauce from pan over chicken; surround with garlic croutons topped with poached eggs. Sprinkle with chopped parsley. Makes 4 servings.

## Chicken Pie

| | |
|---|---|
| 1 (3-pound) chicken | 5 tablespoons milk |
| 1 teaspoon salt | 1 (10-ounce) package frozen |
| ¼ teaspoon pepper | peas |
| 1 bay leaf | 3 tablespoons shortening |
| 2 cups water | 1 small egg, lightly beaten |
| ¼ cup butter | Slices of cucumber for garnish |
| 3½ cups flour | |

Wash chicken; pat dry. Place in a 3-quart glass casserole. Add salt, pepper, bay leaf, and 2 cups of water. Cover and microwave on high for 15 minutes. Turn chicken and cook on low setting for 40 minutes or until chicken is tender. Drain chicken, reserve stock, and cool.

Melt 1/4 cup butter in a medium glass bowl on high for 20 seconds. Add 1/2 cup flour and blend thoroughly; cook for 2 minutes, stirring twice. Gradually stir 2 cups of broth into flour mixture. Heat on high for 2 to 3 minutes, until boiling.

Remove chicken meat from bones and cut up. Mix with sauce and stir in peas. Season with salt and pepper.

Sift rest of flour and a pinch of salt into a mixing bowl. Add remaining margarine and shortening. Cut with 2 knives or a pastry blender until mixture resembles cornmeal. Add just enough cold water to make a stiff dough. Roll out 2/3 of dough; line an 8-inch baking dish.

Spoon filling into dish. Roll out rest of dough and use as a lid for the pie. Trim and decorate edge. Reroll trimmings and cut out shapes to decorate top of pie. Brush with beaten egg and microwave on roast setting for 9 minutes. Transfer to preheated conventional oven at 450°F and bake 10 to 15 minutes, or until golden brown. Makes 6 servings.

## Roast Turkey

| | |
|---|---|
| 1 (10-pound) turkey (there will be enough for sandwiches the next day) | 3 tablespoons shortening |
| | 1 tablespoon paprika |
| | 10 strips bacon |

Truss the turkey; dry the skin with paper towels. Rub shortening over skin and sprinkle with paprika. Cover skin with bacon strips, holding them in place with toothpicks. Cook turkey, breast-side-down, uncovered, on a microwave oven roasting rack or on 2 inverted saucers set in a glass baking dish, for 30 minutes on roast setting.

Turn turkey breast-side-up. Cover leg and wing tips with lightweight aluminum foil to prevent them from overcooking. Rotate turkey 1/4 of a turn and continue cooking for 30 minutes. The internal temperature should read 175°F. It will rise 20 degrees as it rests. Let turkey rest for 15 minutes before carving. Makes 6 servings.

*Sole Fillets with Vegetables*

## Spatchcock Turkey

| | | | |
|---|---|---|---|
| 2 | turkey legs and thighs, cut at joint into serving pieces | ¼ | cup chutney |
| 2 | teaspoons poultry seasoning | 1 | tablespoon catsup |
| 1 | teaspoon salt | 1 | lemon, juiced |
| 2 | lemons, thinly sliced | ¼ | cup soft brown sugar |
| | | 4 | whole fresh tomatoes |
| | | 4 | potatoes, baked or sautéed |

Rub poultry seasoning and salt into turkey. Cover each with lemon slices. In a small glass bowl or casserole, combine chutney, catsup, lemon juice, and sugar. On low, microwave 1 or 2 minutes, until bubbling. Spoon over turkey joints and cook uncovered on roast setting for 20 minutes.

Serve with baked tomatoes and baked or sautéed potatoes. Tomato skins must be pierced in several places before cooking in microwave oven. Garnish with lemon slices and parsley. Makes 4 servings.


## Turkey Tourangelle

| | | | |
|---|---|---|---|
| ¼ | cup butter | ¼ | cup dry white wine |
| ½ | cup onions, finely chopped | 1 | can cream of mushroom soup |
| 1 | cup fresh mushrooms, sliced | ½ | cup sour cream |
| 1 | teaspoon salt | 2 | cups white turkey meat, cooked and sliced |
| ¼ | teaspoon white pepper | | |

Place butter in covered shallow glass baking dish; microwave on medium 2 minutes to melt butter. Add onions; microwave on high 2 minutes. Stir. Add mushrooms and seasonings. Cover; microwave on high 3 minutes.

Add wine to mushroom soup; beat until well mixed. Add to sautéed vegetables; cook, covered, on high 4 minutes. Add sour cream. Gently stir to mix sauce ingredients. Remove from oven.

Place turkey on shallow tray; microwave on high 3 to 4 minutes or until heated thoroughly. Arrange turkey on serving platter; cover with sauce. Makes 4 servings.

*Shrimp Curry*

## Striped Bass

| | | | |
|---|---|---|---|
| 1 | pound striped bass, cleaned and bones removed | ½ | cup cucumber, diced |
| 2 | scallions, finely chopped | ¼ | teaspoon tarragon or 1 tablespoon parsley, chopped |
| 1 | small tomato, peeled, seeded, and chopped | 2 | tablespoons butter |
| | | 1 | tablespoon lemon juice |

Place bass on a piece of waxed paper large enough to enclose it completely. Top fish with all remaining ingredients. Fold long sides of the paper over the fish and tuck the edges beneath, forming a tidy package. Place on inverted plates and microwave for 6 minutes on high. Rotate fish 1/4 of a turn after 3 minutes. Makes 2 servings.

## Braised Halibut in Cream and White Wine

| | |
|---|---|
| 3 **pounds halibut** | ½ **cup cream** |
| 4 **scallions, finely chopped** | ½ **cup white wine** |
| 2 **carrots, thinly sliced** | 1½ **tablespoons flour** |
| 2 **stalks celery, thinly sliced** | **Salt and pepper** |
| ½ **teaspoon thyme** | 2 **tablespoons parsley,** |
| **Grated rind of 1 lemon** | **freshly chopped** |
| 2 **tablespoons butter** | |

Place fish in a 10-inch glass or ceramic baking dish. Arrange vegetables around sides of the dish. Sprinkle fish with thyme and grated lemon rind. Dot with 1 tablespoon of butter. Pour in cream and wine. Cover with waxed paper and microwave on roast setting for 12 minutes. Rotate dish 1/4 of a turn after 6 minutes. Transfer fish to a hot platter and season with salt and pepper. Allow to stand for 5 minutes. It should flake easily, indicating it is completely cooked.

Heat remaining 1 tablespoon of butter in a 6-cup glass measuring cup on high for 20 seconds; then stir butter into the vegetables and liquid in baking dish. Cook for 5 minutes on same setting. Spoon sauce over fish and garnish with parsley. Makes 6 servings.

## "Broiled" Salmon

| | |
|---|---|
| 2 **tablespoons butter** | **Salt and pepper** |
| 1 **(6-ounce) salmon steak** | **Mock Hollandaise Sauce (see** |
| 2 **teaspoons lemon juice** | **next recipe)** |
| **Sprig of parsley** | |

Preheat a microwave browning dish for 3 minutes; add half of the butter. Place salmon on the buttered plate and dot surface with remaining butter. Sprinkle with lemon juice and add the parsley sprig. Cook for 2 minutes on high. Rotate dish 1/4 of a turn and cook for another 2 minutes. Season with salt and pepper. Makes 1 serving.

**Note:** If you are cooking two salmon steaks, cook them 3 minutes on the first side and 2 minutes on the second side.

## Mock Hollandaise Sauce

| | |
|---|---|
| 8 **tablespoons butter** | ¼ **cup mayonnaise** |
| 3 **egg yolks** | **Salt and pepper** |
| 2 **tablespoons lemon juice** | **Dash cayenne pepper** |

Cut butter into small pieces and heat in a 4-cup glass measuring cup on high for 50 seconds, until hot and bubbling. Stir in egg yolks, lemon juice, and mayonnaise, stirring rapidly with a small wire whisk. Return to oven for 50 seconds. Stir rapidly after 25 seconds and immediately after it is taken from the oven. Season with salt, pepper, and cayenne. Makes 4 servings.

*Seafood Rissoto*

## Poached Cod with Lemon Sauce

| | |
|---|---|
| 1 **pound cod fillets** | ***Lemon Sauce*** |
| **Seasoned salt and pepper** | 1 **tablespoon butter or** |
| 1 **tablespoon lemon juice** | **margarine** |
| 2 **shallots, peeled and** | ¾ **cup mayonnaise** |
| **chopped** | **Juice of ½ lemon** |
| ¼ **cup white wine** | ½ **teaspoon dry mustard** |
| 1 **tablespoon butter or** | ½ **teaspoon salt** |
| **margarine** | ½ **tablespoon capers,** |
| | **chopped** |

Wash fish; pat dry. Lightly sprinkle with seasoned salt and pepper. Sprinkle with lemon juice. Place fillets in 9-inch-square casserole with thickest portion toward outside of dish. Sprinkle with shallots; pour wine over all. Dot with butter. Cover tightly; cook on high 5 to 6 minutes or until fish flakes with fork. Let stand covered while making sauce.

Melt butter for sauce in 2-cup glass measuring cup by microwaving on high 45 seconds. Add mayonnaise, lemon juice, mustard, and salt; stir well. Microwave on low 3 minutes or until just heated through. Stir once. Do not overcook or boil; mixture will curdle. Stir in capers.

Place fish on warm platter; add sauce. Garnish with lemon slices and whole capers. Serve. Makes 4 servings.


## Flounder Rolls with Shrimp Sauce

| | |
|---|---|
| 1 **pound small flounder** | ½ **teaspoon salt** |
| **fillets (or fillet of sole)** | ½ **tablespoon butter** |
| 2 **tablespoons butter or** | 2 **tablespoons flour** |
| **margarine** | 1 **tablespoon lemon juice** |
| ½ **cup fresh mushrooms,** | 2 **tablespoons butter, melted** |
| **finely chopped** | ½ **(10¾-ounce) can cream of** |
| 1 **shallot, peeled and minced** | **shrimp soup** |
| 1 **cup small shrimp, chopped** | 3 **tablepoons dry sherry** |
| **and cooked** | **Pimiento slivers** |
| ¼ **cup water** | |

Wash fish fillets; pat dry.

Place 2 tablespoons butter in measuring cup; microwave on high 45 seconds. Add mushrooms and shallot; microwave on high 2 minutes. Add shrimp; stir well. Set aside.

Combine water, salt, and 1/2 tablespoon butter in dish or measuring cup; microwave on high 1-1/2 minutes. Add flour; mix rapidly to form smooth paste. Combine flour paste and mushroom mixture. Spread 1 side of fillet with shrimp and mushroom mixture; roll up to form pinwheel. Secure with wooden pick. Place close together in small shallow glass casserole. Drizzle with lemon juice and melted butter. Cover tightly with plastic wrap; microwave on high 4 minutes. Let stand 5 minutes.

*Spanish Eggs*

Combine soup and sherry in sauceboat; microwave on high 1-1/2 minutes. Garnish fish with pimiento. Serve accompanied by sauce. Makes 4 servings.

## Sole Fillets with Vegetables

| | |
|---|---|
| 1 **tablespoon butter** | ½ **teaspoon salt** |
| 1 **stalk celery, thinly sliced** | ¾ **cup heavy cream** |
| 1 **scallion, thinly sliced** | 2 **sole fillets (about 1** |
| 2 **carrots, thinly slicecd** | **pound)** |

Melt butter in medium baking dish 20 seconds on high. Add vegetable slices and salt; cook 2 minutes. While stirring rapidly, add cream; cook 3 minutes.

Add sole; cook 3 minutes. Remove sole; set on serving plate. Cook sauce 1 additional minute. Take out of oven. Pour sauce over slices of sole Makes 2 servings.

## Seafood Quiche Lorraine

**Pastry**
1¼ cups flour
6 tablespoons butter
3 tablespoons cold water
3 tablespoons light cream

**Cheese Filling**
3 eggs
1¼ cups Gruyère cheese, grated
¼ cup Parmesan cheese, grated

¾ cup milk
½ cup light cream
¼ teaspoon paprika or white pepper
⅛ teaspoon nutmeg
½ teaspoon salt
For shellfish choose among: 4 ounces shrimp, crab, or lobster

To make pastry, sift flour into a bowl. Cut in butter with a knife or pastry blender until mixture looks mealy. Make a hole in the center and pour water and cream into it. Work pastry with a spoon until it can be formed into a ball. Chill thoroughly. Roll out to fit an 8- or 9-inch glass pie plate. Flute edge; prick bottom and sides of crust with fork. Cook on roast setting for 7 minutes.

To make filling, beat the eggs. Add cheeses, milk, cream, seasonings, and spices. Arrange shellfish, cleaned and shelled, in pie shell. Pour cream mixture into pie shell and cook on defrost setting for 30 to 35 minutes, or until a knife inserted in center comes out clean. Let quiche stand 5 minutes before serving. Makes 6 servings.

## Shrimp Curry

1½ pounds medium-sized fresh shrimp
2 tablespoons oil
1 onion, finely chopped
½ green pepper, finely chopped
1 tablespoon curry powder
¼ teaspoon cumin

Dash of cayenne pepper
2 tablespoons flour
1½ cups chicken broth
1 teaspoon lemon juice
1 tablespoon tomato paste
Toasted Coconut (optional; see below)

Peel and devein shrimp; set aside. Heat oil in 1-1/2-quart glass or ceramic casserole on high 30 seconds. Add onion and green pepper; cook 1 minute. Stir in curry powder, cumin, and cayenne; cook 20 seconds. Stir in flour. Using wire whisk, stir in chicken broth, lemon juice, and tomato paste; cook 3 minutes. Add shrimp; cook 3 minutes.

Sprinkle with Toasted Coconut. Serve with rice and chutney. Makes 4 servings.

**To make Toasted Coconut:** Spread 1 cup grated coconut on paper plate; cook, uncovered, on high 2 minutes. Stir; cook 1 minute. Sprinkle part of coconut over shrimp; serve rest in separate bowl.

*Deviled Eggs Mornay*

## Seafood Rissoto

| | |
|---|---|
| ½ **pound medium-sized shrimp** | ¼ **cup butter** |
| | 1 **small onion, chopped** |
| **Stock Ingredients** | 2 **cups uncooked rice** |
| 2 **small onions, sliced** | 1 **stalk celery, chopped** |
| ½ **stalk celery** | 1 **red pepper, sliced** |
| 1 **clove garlic** | 1 **package frozen green peas** |
| 1 **cup white wine** | ¼ **teaspoon saffron** |
| ½ **teaspoon salt** | 2 **tablespoons parsley, finely chopped** |
| ¼ **teaspoon pepper** | ¼ **cup Parmesan cheese, grated** |

Peel and devein shrimp. Put stock ingredients plus shrimp peels and 2-1/2 cups water in a 1-1/2-quart glass or ceramic casserole. Microwave on high for 5 minutes. Strain.

Melt butter in a 2-1/2-quart casserole for 20 seconds. Add onion and cook for 2 minutes, until transparent. Add rice and stir well. Pour in strained stock. Cook for 12 minutes. Rotate dish 1/4 turn every 2 minutes. Add celery, red pepper, thawed peas, mushrooms, shrimp, and ground saffron. Cover casserole and cook 6 minutes on high, until shrimp are pink. Stir mixture and rotate dish 1/4 of a turn after 3 minutes. Before serving, sprinkle with parsley and grated Parmesan cheese. Makes 4 servings.

## Spanish Eggs

| | |
|---|---|
| 1 **tablespoon butter or margarine** | ½ **cup frozen red and green peppers, chopped** |
| 1 **shallot, peeled and chopped** | 1 **cup chorizo, linginica, or other hot sausage (or substitute ham), chopped** |
| 1 **cup potato, peeled and diced** | **Salt and pepper to taste** |
| 2 **medium canned tomatoes, drained and chopped** | 2 **eggs** |
| | **Chopped parsley** |

Place butter in 1-quart casserole dish with lid. Microwave, uncovered, on high 45 seconds. Add vegetables, sausage, and seasonings; stir well. Cover; microwave on high 5 to 7 minutes, stirring once, or until potatoes are tender. Make 2 wells in vegetable mixture.

Break eggs, 1 at a time, into sauce dish; slide into wells in vegetable mixture. Cover; microwave on high 1 minute and 40 seconds. Let stand, covered, 3 minutes. Eggs should be set.

Garnish eggs with chopped parsley. Serve with corn muffins. Makes 2 servings.

*Frittata*

## Deviled Eggs Mornay

| | |
|---|---|
| 2 tablespoons butter | 1 cup cooked pasta shells |
| 2 tablespoons flour | 6 hard-boiled eggs |
| 1¼ cups milk | 1 teaspoon dry mustard |
| ½ teaspoon salt | ½ teaspoon curry powder |
| ¼ teaspoon pepper | 2 tablespoons butter, melted |
| 1½ cups Cheddar cheese, grated | 3 or 4 green olives, sliced |
| | 3 or 4 tablespoons cream |

Melt butter in a 1-quart measuring glass for 20 seconds on the high. Stir in flour with a wire whisk; stir in milk gradually. Cook for 3 minutes or until thick. During cooking, stir twice with whisk to give a smooth sauce. Season with salt and pepper. Add 1/2 cup of grated cheese and the cooked pasta. Place in an ovenproof dish and keep it warm in a conventional oven.

Cut eggs in half lengthwise and remove yolks. Mix yolks with mustard, curry powder, melted butter, and salt and pepper to taste. Put mixture into egg-white halves. Cover with sauce. Arrange sliced olives on top of sauce. Top with and sprinkle with remaining cheese. Microwave uncovered on high for 2 minutes to melt cheese. Serve immediately. Makes 4 servings.

*Asparagus with White Sauce*

## Frittata

| | | | |
|---|---|---|---|
| 1 | small fresh tomato | 3 | eggs |
| 2 | tablespoons butter or margarine | 3 | tablespoons water |
| 2 | tablespoons onion, chopped | ¼ | teaspoon dried sweet basil, crumbled |
| 2 | tablespoons green pepper, chopped (optional) | | Salt and pepper |
| ½ | cup zucchini, thinly sliced | 1 | ounce provolone or mozzarella cheese, thinly sliced |

Prick tomato lightly with fork. Place on paper towel; microwave on high 30 seconds. Let stand 5 minutes. Peel; coarsely chop.

Place butter in 9-inch glass pie plate; microwave on high 45 seconds. Add onion, green pepper, and zucchini; stir well. Distribute vegetables evenly in dish; microwave on high 2 minutes.

Meanwhile, beat eggs, water, basil, salt, and pepper. Pour egg mixture over vegetables; cover with plastic wrap. Cook on medium 2-1/2 minutes. Stir in tomato; cover. Cook 1-1/2 minutes. Uncover; top with cheese. Re-cover; microwave on high 1/2 minute. Let stand 2 minutes.

Cut frittata in wedges and serve. Makes 4 servings.

# Vegetables and Rice

## Asparagus with Cashew Cream

| | |
|---|---|
| 1 **(10-ounce) package frozen asparagus spears** | *Sauce* |
| 2 **tablespoons dry sherry** | 1½ **tablespoons butter or margarine** |
| **Salt and pepper** | 1½ **tablespoons flour** |
| 1 **tablespoon butter or margarine** | 1 **tablespoon soy sauce** |
| | ¾ **cup buttermilk** |
| | ½ **cup mayonnaise** |
| | **Dash of cayenne pepper** |
| | ¼ **cup roasted cashews** |

Place asparagus in 1-1/2-quart casserole. Pour sherry over asparagus; sprinkle with salt and pepper. Dot with 1 tablespoon butter. Cover with lid or plastic wrap; microwave on high 6 or 7 minutes. Let stand 5 minutes.

To make sauce, place 1-1/2 tablespoons butter in large glass measuring cup; microwave on high 40 seconds to melt. Add flour; microwave on high 40 seconds. Stir in soy sauce and buttermilk; mix well. Microwave on high 1-1/2 minutes, stirring once. Stir in mayonnaise and cayenne pepper. Microwave on low 1-1/2 minutes to heat through.

Arrange asparagus on serving platter. Pour sauce over all; sprinkle with cashews. Serve immediately. Makes 2 to 3 servings.

## Asparagus with White Sauce

| | |
|---|---|
| 2 **pounds uniform-sized fresh asparagus spears** | **White Sauce** |
| ½ **cup cold water** | 2 **tablespoons butter** |
| 1 **tablespoon lemon juice** | 2 **tablespoons flour** |
| 1 **teaspoon salt** | ¾ **cup milk** |
| 1 **tablespoon butter** | ¾ **cup light cream** |
| | ⅛ **teaspoon nutmeg** |
| | **Salt and pepper** |
| | 2 **hard-boiled eggs** |

Trim the asparagus and place in a baking dish. Add water, lemon juice, and salt. Cover with waxed paper and microwave on high for 6 minutes. Drain and immediately rinse under cold running water. Place on a serving dish, dot with 1 tablespoon of butter, and keep asparagus warm while preparing sauce.

Heat 2 tablespoons of butter in a 4-cup measuring glass for 30 seconds on high. Stir in flour, milk, cream, nutmeg, salt, and pepper, and cook for 3 minutes. Stir with a wire whisk twice to ensure a smooth sauce. Reserve 1 egg yolk. Chop remaining yolk and whites and add to hot sauce. Place sauce in sauce boat and sprinkle with remaining chopped egg yolk. Reheat asparagus for 1-1/2 minutes just before serving with the sauce. Makes 6 servings.

## Green Beans with Parmesan Cheese

| | |
|---|---|
| 1½ **pounds string beans** | 2 **tablespoons butter** |
| ¼ **cup water** | 2 **tablespoons parsley, finely chopped** |
| 1 **teaspoon salt** | **Freshly ground black pepper** |
| ¼ **cup Parmesan cheese, freshly grated** | |

Trim and wash beans. Place in a shallow 10-inch glass dish and add water and salt. Cover with waxed paper and microwave for 8 minutes on high. Drain and rinse immediately under cold running water. Return to dish and sprinkle with cheese. Dot with butter. Cook uncovered for 2 minutes. Sprinkle with finely chopped parsley and season with pepper. Makes 4 servings.

*Confetti Corn*

## Confetti Corn

| | | | |
|---|---|---|---|
| 2 | tablespoons butter or margarine | 1 | (10-ounce) package frozen whole-kernel corn |
| 2 | tablespoons onion, finely minced | Salt and pepper to taste | |
| ¼ | cup frozen green and red pepper, finely chopped | 1 | tablespoon parsley, finely chopped |

Place butter into 1-quart casserole; microwave on high 45 seconds. Add onion and stir well. Microwave on high 2 minutes. Stir in peppers and corn; cover tightly. Cook on high 4 to 6 minutes or until tender. Let stand 5 minutes.

Season with salt and pepper to taste; sprinkle with chopped parsley. Makes 4 servings.

## Stuffed Cabbage Leaves

| | |
|---|---|
| 1 **medium-sized cabbage** | ¼ **teaspoon allspice** |
| 1 **tablespoon oil** | ½ **teaspoon cinnamon** |
| 1 **onion, finely chopped** | 1 **teaspoon salt** |
| 1 **pound ground chuck steak** | **Freshly ground black pepper** |
| 1½ **cups cooked rice** | ½ **cup beef broth** |
| 1 **tablespoon tomato paste** | 1 **cup tomato sauce** |
| ¼ **cup parsley, finely chopped** | |

Place cabbage in a 3-quart glass or ceramic casserole. Add 1/2 cup cold water, cover, and microwave 4 minutes on high, until the leaves can be loosened easily. Discard tough outer leaves and select 12 or 14 large perfect leaves. Remove heavy stems. (Use remaining cabbage for another meal.)

Heat oil in a 2-quart glass bowl in the microwave oven for 20 seconds. Add onion and microwave 1 minute on high. Add ground beef and cook for 3 minutes. Break up beef with a fork and rotate dish 1/4 of a turn after 1-1/2 minutes. Combine onion and beef with the rice, tomato paste, parsley, allspice, cinnamon, salt, and pepper.

Place a little of the mixture in center of each leaf. Fold sides over and roll leaves to form tidy packages. Place seam-side-down in a 12-inch glass baking dish. Add beef broth and tomato sauce. Cover with waxed paper and microwave for 8 minutes on high. Rotate dish , 1/4 of a turn after 3 minutes. Makes 6 servings.

## Wilted Cabbage

| | |
|---|---|
| 1 **(2-pound) head cabbage** | ⅔ **cup water** |
| 2 **tablespoons pimiento-stuffed olives, sliced** | 1 **tablespoon flour** |
| | 2 **tablespoons sugar** |
| | ½ **teaspoon dry mustard** |
| ***Hot Bacon Dressing*** | **Pinch of salt** |
| 4 **slices bacon** | 1 **egg, well beaten** |
| ⅓ **cup vinegar** | |

Cut stem and core out of cabbage. Blanch whole cabbage in boiling water 5 minutes. Drain; rinse in cold water. Fold back outer leaves; hollow out center. Coarsely shred cabbage removed from shell.

Place bacon slices side by side in 10-inch-square casserole or microwave browning dish. Microwave on high 3 to 3-1/2 minutes or until crisp, rearranging once. Remove from pan; drain on paper towels. Add vinegar and water to bacon drippings. Cover; cook on high 2 minutes, until mixture boils.

Meanwhile, combine flour, sugar and mustard; mix well. Slowly stir flour mixture into boiling liquid. Cover; cook on high 3 minutes, until thickened, stirring once. Quickly stir in beaten egg; mix well. Egg will cook in hot liquid, forming thin strings. Crumble reserved bacon; stir into dressing.

Combine shredded cabbage with bacon dressing. Stuff shell with cabbage mixture. Garnish with olives. Place in serving dish; cover. Microwave on high 2 minutes to heat through. Makes 4 servings.

*Peas French-Style*

*Acorn Squash with Apples*

## Onions Monte Carlo

| | |
|---|---|
| 1 tablespoon oil | 2 tablespoons flour |
| 1 tablespoon butter | 1 cup beef broth |
| 1½ pounds small white onions, peeled, with cross cut in each root end | 1 cup red wine |
| | 1 tablespoon tomato paste |
| | ¼ teaspoon thyme |
| 1 tablespoon sugar | ½ teaspoon salt |

Heat microwave browning plate 4 minutes. Add oil and butter; brown onions on high 4 minutes. Sprinkle with sugar. Stir onions; cook 1-1/2 minutes.

Transfer to 1-1/2-quart glass or ceramic casserole. Stir flour into onions; add remaining ingredients. Cover; cook 10 minutes, until onions are tender. Makes 8 servings.

## Rice

| | | | |
|---|---|---|---|
| 2 | cups boiling water | 1 | tablespoon butter |
| ½ | teaspoon salt | 1 | cup long-grain rice |

Pour water into a 1-quart glass casserole. Add remaining ingredients. Cover and microwave on high for 10 minutes. Remove from oven and let stand for 10 minutes. Makes 6 servings.

**Note:** To reheat rice, place it in a small casserole. Cover and cook 1 minute.

## Spinach Tarts

| | | | |
|---|---|---|---|
| 1½ cups flour | | 5 | tablespoons sour cream |
| Pinch of salt | | 1 | large egg |
| 3 | tablespoons butter | 1 | teaspoon grated nutmeg |
| 1 | tablespoon shortening | Salt and pepper to taste | |
| 4 or 5 tablespoons water | | | |
| 1 | (10-ounce) package frozen chopped spinach | | |

Sift flour and salt into a bowl. Cut in butter and shortening with 2 knives or a pastry blender until mixture resembles cornmeal. Add water to make a firm pastry dough. Chill at least 1 hour before rolling out. Use 6 to 8 glass custard cups for tart pans. Line with pastry, and flute edges.

Cook spinach according to package directions. Drain and puree in a blender. Combine sour cream, egg, and spinach. Season to taste with nutmeg, salt, and pepper. Spoon into pastry and cook 3 cups at a time on defrost or lowest setting for 12 minutes or until knife inserted near center comes out clean. Test every 2 minutes during end of cooking period. Tarts will not brown without special browning unit. Makes 6 to 8 servings.

## Mushroom Caps

| | | | |
|---|---|---|---|
| ½ | cup butter | 20 | large mushroom caps |
| ¼ | teaspoon garlic salt | 4 | slices homemade bread, sliced thick |
| 2 | spring onions | | |

Microwave butter on high 1 minute or until melted. Stir in garlic salt. Chop green onions; add to butter. Clean mushroom caps; arrange in single layer in glass casserole dish. Pour seasoned butter over mushrooms. Cover; cook on high 2 minutes.

Toast bread on both sides. Using decorative round cookie cutter, cut out centers of toast slices. Arrange mushroom caps on top of bread slices. Pour butter over mushrooms. Serve immediately. Makes 4 servings.

## Mushrooms with Cheese Sauce

| | | | |
|---|---|---|---|
| 8 | large mushrooms | 2 | tablespoons flour |
| 3 | slices bacon | 1¼ | cups milk |
| 1 | tablespoon butter | ¼ | cup Swiss cheese, grated |
| 4 | scallions, finely chopped | ½ | cup bread crumbs |
| 1 | clove garlic, finely chopped | ¼ | cup Parmesan cheese, grated |

Remove stems from mushrooms and chop them finely. Fry bacon in an 8-inch glass baking dish on high setting for 3 minutes, until the fat is rendered. Remove and crumble bacon. Add butter to the bacon fat and brown mushroom caps for 1-1/2 minutes.

Remove the mushroom caps and microwave the chopped stems, scallions, and garlic for 1-1/2 minutes, also on high. Stir in flour and cook 30 seconds. Stir in milk and cook 2 minutes. Stir in grated Swiss cheese; cook 50 seconds.

Return mushroom caps and crumbled bacon to baking dish. Top with bread crumbs and grated Parmesan cheese. Place under a preheated broiler for 3 minutes. The crumbs will not brown in the microwave oven unless you have a model with a browning attachment. Makes 4 servings.

## Peas French-Style

| | | | |
|---|---|---|---|
| | Outer leaves of garden or iceberg lettuce | ½ | teaspoon salt |
| 1 | (10-ounce) package frozen peas | ½ | teaspoon sugar |
| ½ | cup frozen small whole onions or 8 small whole onions, peeled and slashed on ends | 2 | tablespoons sauterne or dry sherry |

Line 2-quart glass casserole with lettuce leaves. Combine peas, onions, seasonings, and wine; pour into lettuce-lined casserole. Cover tightly with plastic wrap. Microwave on high 5 to 6 minutes. Let stand 5 minutes. Serve immediately. Makes 4 servings.

*Stuffed Tomatoes*

## Green Peas Bonne Femme

| | | | |
|---|---|---|---|
| ¼ | **pound bacon, cut in 1-inch pieces** | ½ | **cup water** |
| | | ½ | **teaspoon salt** |
| 2 | **tablespoons butter** | ¼ | **teaspoon pepper** |
| 3 | **cups fresh green peas** | 1 | **tablespoon sugar** |
| 6 | **small white onions** | 1 | **tablespoon parsley, finely** |
| **Inner leaves of a lettuce** | | | **chopped** |

Fry bacon in a 1-quart glass casserole on high for 3 minutes. Add butter, peas, onions, lettuce, water, salt, and pepper. Cover and microwave on high for 10 minutes. Add sugar after 8 minutes.

When peas are done, drain remaining liquid. Sprinkle with parsley before serving. Makes 6 servings.

## Acorn Squash with Apples

| | | | |
|---|---|---|---|
| 1 | medium acorn squash | 2 | tablespoons brown sugar |
| Salt | | 2 | tablespoons butter or |
| 1 | fresh tart apple, peeled, | | margarine |
| | cored, quartered, and | ¼ | teaspoon ground |
| | sliced | | cinnamon |

Split squash in half lengthwise; remove seeds and membranes. Wash; pat dry. Place into shallow casserole. Salt lightly and cover with waxed paper. Microwave on high 3 minutes. Remove from oven; rotate position of squash halves.

Fill cavity in each half with apple slices. Sprinkle each half with 1 tablespoon brown sugar; dot with 1 tablespoon butter. Sprinkle each half with 1/8 teaspoon cinnamon. Cover and cook on high 4 to 5 minutes or until tender. Serve hot. Makes 2 servings.

## Stuffed Tomatoes

| | | | |
|---|---|---|---|
| 8 | fresh tomatoes | 2 | cups cooked ham, |
| 3 | tablespoons butter | | chopped |
| 1 | small onion, finely | ½ | cup fresh bread crumbs |
| | chopped | ¼ | cup Parmesan cheese |
| ¼ | cup green pepper | 1 | teaspoon paprika |
| 1 | cup fresh mushrooms, | | |
| | chopped | | |

Cut tops off tomatoes; scoop out insides. Save pulp for soup. Turn tomatoes upside down; drain. Arrange in glass baking dish.

Combine 1 tablespoon butter, onion, and green pepper in covered glass dish. Microwave on high 4 minutes, stirring once during cooking process. Add mushrooms and ham; cook on medium 4 minutes, stirring once during cooking process. Fill tomato shells with ham and mushroom mixture.

Microwave 2 tablespoons butter in glass dish on medium 1-1/2 minutes. Stir in bread crumbs, cheese and paprika; mix well. Top tomatoes with crumb mixture. Place tomatoes uncovered in microwave; cook on high 8 to 10 minutes or until heated thoroughly. Cover loosely with aluminum foil; let stand 3 minutes before serving. Makes 8 servings.

# Breads and Desserts

## *Apple Brown Betty*

| | |
|---|---|
| **3 cups bread crumbs made from Italian or French bread** | **½ cup butter** |
| **¾ cup sugar** | **4 medium-sized cooking apples, peeled, cored, and very thinly sliced** |
| **⅛ teaspoon nutmeg, freshly grated** | **½ cup raisins** |
| **1 teaspoon cinnamon** | **½ cup water** |

Form bread into crumbs in blender. Heat microwave browning plate for 4 minutes on high. Add 2 tablespoons of butter and cook for 30 seconds, until melted. Spread half the crumbs in an even layer on plate. Cook for 1 minute; stir. Cook for 1 minute more, until crumbs are lightly browned and crisp. Repeat with remaining crumbs. Stir together crumbs, sugar, and spices.

Butter a 2-quart soufflé dish or similar bowl. Place a layer of 1/3 of the crumbs in the bowl. Place raisins in a 1-cup glass measuring cup and cover with 1/2 cup water. Cook in microwave oven for 1 minute and drain.

Top the layer of bread crumbs with a layer of half the apples and raisins. Add a layer of crumbs, then the remaining apples and raisins. Finish with a top layer of crumbs. Dot with remaining butter and microwave on roast setting for 10 minutes. Makes 6 servings.

## Stuffed Baked Apples

| | |
|---|---|
| 6 | **large cooking apples** |
| 3 | **tablespoons dates, chopped** |
| 3 | **tablespoons walnuts, chopped** |

| | |
|---|---|
| ¼ | **cup honey** |
| 1 | **(10-ounce) jar red currant jelly** |

Core apples. Cut skin of apples around centers; do not remove. Combine dates, walnuts, and honey; mix well. Arrange apples in glass baking dish. Fill centers with date-nut mixture. Microwave on high 10 to 12 minutes or until apples are tender. Remove from oven. Remove upper halves of apple skins.

Place jelly in microwave; heat on high 3 minutes or until jelly melts. Spoon over apples. Makes 6 servings.

## Banana Ice-Cream Layers

| | |
|---|---|
| 1½ | **cups all-purpose flour** |
| ½ | **teaspoon baking powder** |
| ½ | **teaspoon baking soda** |
| ¼ | **teaspoon salt** |
| ½ | **cup margarine** |
| ½ | **cup brown sugar** |
| ½ | **cup granulated sugar** |
| 2 | **eggs, beaten** |

| | |
|---|---|
| 1 | **teaspoon vanilla** |
| ¾ | **cup ripe bananas, mashed** |
| 2 | **tablespoons lemon yogurt** |
| 1½ | **cups strawberry yogurt** |
| 1½ | **cups vanilla ice cream** |
| 1 | **cup sweetened whipped cream** |
| ½ | **cup apricot preserves** |

Combine flour, baking powder, baking soda, and salt; mix well. Cream margarine until fluffy. Add sugars; blend until smooth. Add eggs and vanilla; mix until blended. Add bananas and yogurts; beat until batter is well-blended. Stir in dry mixture.

Line bottom of 9-inch loaf glass baking dish with waxed paper. Pour in batter; bake on medium 15 minutes, rotating dish 1/2 turn each 5 minutes, to raise batter. Change microwave setting to high; flash cake 2 to 3 minutes to set cake. Let cake set 5 minutes before removing from pan. Cool completely.

Soften ice cream by flashing on low 20 to 30 seconds; whip to allow for easy spreading. Slice cake lengthwise into 5 equal layers. Spread ice cream alternately between cake layers; stack. Decorate top of cake with whipped cream.

Microwave preserves on high 20 seconds to 1 minute to soften; drizzle over top of cake. Serve immediately. Makes 12 servings.

*Stuffed Baked Apples*

## French Apple Flan

| | | | |
|---|---|---|---|
| ¼ | cup butter | 1 | cup flour |
| ½ | cup sugar | 4 | large cooking apples |
| 2 | large egg yolks | 3 | tablespoons apricot jam, strained |
| ½ | teaspoon vanilla extract or essence | | |

Combine butter, 1/4 cup sugar, and egg yolks and work together with fingers until smooth. Add vanilla extract and mix well. Work in flour and knead to form a smooth dough. Form into a ball and put into a plastic bag. Chill for 30 minutes and roll out to fit an 8- or 9-inch glass pie plate. Prick bottom and sides of crust with fork. Microwave on roast setting for 6 minutes.

Meanwhile, wash, peel, core, and thinly slice cooking apples. Place 1/3 of the apple slices in pastry shell; sprinkle on 2 tablespoons of remaining sugar. Repeat. Arrange remaining apples in an attractive ring on top. Cook on high for 7 minutes or until apples are soft. Remove from oven.

Heat apricot jam in a small custard cup on high for 1 minute. Brush jam over flan while hot. Makes 6 servings.

## Banana-Nut Bread

| | | | |
|---|---|---|---|
| ½ | cup butter | ½ | teaspoon baking powder |
| ¾ | cup brown sugar | ½ | teaspoon baking soda |
| 1 | ripe banana, mashed | ½ | teaspoon salt |
| 1 | teaspoon lemon juice | ¼ | teaspoon nutmeg |
| 2 | eggs | ½ | cup pecans, chopped |
| 1¼ | cups flour | | |

Cream butter and sugar together. Mix banana, lemon juice, and eggs. Sift flour, baking powder, baking soda, salt, nutmeg, and pecans together. Combine the 2 mixtures, stirring until flour is just combined.

Bake in an 8-inch square glass or ceramic baking dish lined with waxed paper for 8 minutes on high. Turn dish 1/4 of a turn every 2 minutes. Leave bread in pan for 5 minutes. Transfer to a cooling rack, waxed paper side down, and leave to cool for 10 minutes. Peel off paper and cut into 16 squares. Makes 16 squares.

## Brownies

| | | | |
|---|---|---|---|
| 4 | squares (1 ounce each) unsweetened chocolate | ½ | teaspoon salt |
| 6 | tablespoons butter | ½ | teaspoon baking powder |
| 2 | eggs | 1 | teaspoon vanilla extract |
| 1 | cup sugar | ½ | cup walnuts or pecans, chopped |
| 1 | cup all-purpose flour, sifted | | |

Line an 8 × 8-inch glass baking dish with buttered waxed paper. Break chocolate into small pieces and place in a bowl with the butter. Cook in microwave oven on high for 1 minute 30 seconds, until the chocolate has completely melted.

Beat eggs and sugar together until creamy. Sift flour with salt and baking powder. Stir all ingredients together. Spread mixture evenly into baking dish. Cook for 4-1/2 minutes, rotating dish 1/4 of a turn twice during cooking period. Cool brownies in the dish. Remove paper and cut brownies into squares. Makes 16 squares.

*Banana Ice-Cream Layers*

## Chocolate and Molasses Cake

| | |
|---|---|
| 1 **tablespoon cocoa powder, regular, not instant** | 2 **teaspoons baking soda** |
| ¼ **cup butter** | 2 **tablespoons molasses** |
| ¼ **cup sugar** | ⅓ **cup warm milk** |
| 1 **large egg** | **Optional decoration: candied cherries** |
| 1½ **cups flour** | |

Blend cocoa powder with 3 tablespoons hot water and let cool. Beat butter with sugar until light and fluffy. Gradually add egg, beating well. Mix in cocoa and butter. Sift flour with baking soda. Mix molasses with warm milk. Fold flour and molasses alternately into creamed mixture.

Line bottom of a 9-inch round glass baking dish with waxed paper. Pour mixture into prepared dish. Cook on low for 7 minutes and then on high for 3 to 4 minutes, or until a toothpick inserted in the center comes out clean. Cool for 5 minutes before removing from dish.

Decorate with halves of candied cherries. Makes 6 to 8 servings.

## Chocolate and Orange Cake

| | |
|---|---|
| 1 **cup butter** | 1 **small banana** |
| 1 **cup sugar** | 1 **pineapple ring (from can)** |
| 4 **eggs, beaten** | ¼ **cup chocolate frosting** |
| 1 **orange** | ½ **cup confectioners' sugar** |
| 2 **cups self-rising flour** | **Yellow food coloring** |
| ¾ **cup whipping cream** | |

Line bottoms of 2 round glass baking dishes with waxed paper. Beat butter and sugar together. Add eggs, 1 at a time, beating well. Add grated orange rind; reserve rest of orange. Sift flour and fold into mixture. Spoon into baking dishes and bake 1 at a time. Cook on low for 7 minutes. Continue cooking on high for 3 to 4 minutes, or until toothpick inserted near center comes out clean. Repeat for second layer. Let cake stand 5 minutes before turning out on serving plate.

Whip cream, sweetened to taste, and mix in sliced banana. Section orange and reserve 3 sections. Chop rest and fold into cream; cut pineapple into pieces. Reserve 3 pieces of pineapple and fold remainder into cream. Spread over 1 layer.

Cut other cake into 6 wedges. Frost 3 wedges with chocolate icing. Top with pineapple.

Sift confectioners' sugar; add just enough water to make smooth icing. Add food coloring to color pale yellow and spread on 3 wedges. Decorate with orange. Assemble cake as shown in picture. Refrigerate and serve within a few hours. Makes 6 servings.

*French Apple Flan*

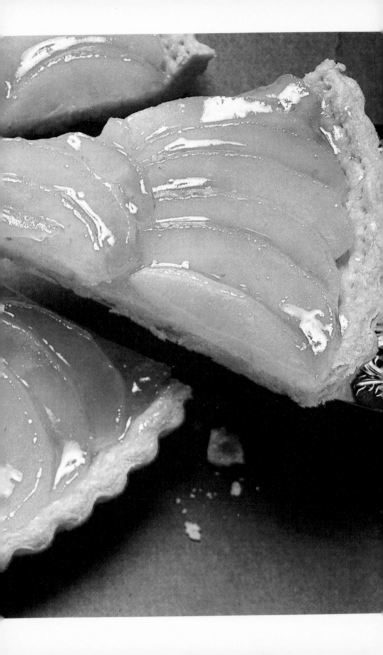

## Jam Layers

| | |
|---|---|
| ½ cup vegetable shortening | 1 teaspoon vanilla |
| 2 cups sugar | 3 egg whites |
| 3 egg yolks | 1 (10-ounce) jar black |
| 2 cups unbleached flour | currant jam |
| 3 teaspoons baking powder | ½ cup powdered sugar |
| 1 cup milk | |

Cream shortening and sugar until light and fluffy. Add egg yolks; beat until well mixed. Combine flour and baking powder. Add to creamed mixture alternately with milk and vanilla, beating well after each addition. Beat egg whites stiff; fold into cake batter.

Fill 2 waxed-paper-lined, 8-inch glass cake pans 1/2 full of batter. Bake each layer individually 7 minutes on medium and 2 minutes, 30 seconds on high, until toothpick inserted in center comes out clean. Let stand 5 minutes before removing from pan. Cool. Bake cupcakes from remaining batter.*

Heat jam on high 1 minute, 30 seconds, until spreadable. Spread between cake layers; stack. Sift powdered sugar on top of cake. Makes 12 cake servings and 6 cupcakes.

* Fill cupcake papers 1/2 full of batter. Put in glass custard cups or microwave cupcake tray; bake as follows:

| cupcakes | time on medium |
|---|---|
| 2 | 2-2-1/2 min. |
| 4 | 2-3/4-3-1/2 min. |
| 6 | 4-1/4-5 min. |

## Victoria Lemon Cake

| | |
|---|---|
| 1 cup sweet butter | 2 cups self-rising flour |
| Grated rind of ½ lemon | 1 to 1½ cups lemon pudding |
| 1 cup sugar | ¼ cup confectioners' sugar |
| 4 eggs | |

Cream butter until soft. Add lemon rind. Gradually beat in sugar until mixture is soft and pale. Beat eggs lightly and stir into mixture a little at a time. Sift flour onto mixture and fold in with a spatula.

Line bottoms of 2 round, medium-sized glass baking dishes with waxed paper. Divide mixture equally between the dishes. Cook 1 at a time on low for 7 minutes and then on high for 3 or 4 minutes, or until toothpick comes out clean. Let cake stand 5 minutes to set. Spread lemon pudding on top of 1 layer and place second layer on top. Sprinkle with confectioners' sugar. Makes 10 to 12 slices.

*Chocolate and Orange Cake*

## Pineapple Gateau

| | |
|---|---|
| 3 **large eggs** | 1 **(16-ounce) can pineapple** |
| ¾ **cup sugar** | **rings** |
| 1 **tablespoon cold water** | 1¼ **cups heavy cream** |
| ¾ **cup flour** | 3 **tablespoons red currant** |
| ¾ **cup cornstarch** | **jelly** |
| 2 **teaspoons baking powder** | |

Beat eggs, sugar, and water for 15 minutes or until very thick and creamy. Sift flour with cornstarch and baking powder. Fold into beaten egg mixture lightly and carefully. Line bottom of a 9-inch round baking dish with waxed paper. Pour mixture into prepared dish. Cook on low for 7 minutes. Continue cooking on high for 3 or 4 minutes, or until a toothpick comes out clean. Let cake stand 5 minutes to set. Turn out on serving plate to cool.

Drain pineapple and chop finely. Whip cream and butter. Put half of cream in a pastry bag fitted with a medium star nozzle. Put red currant jelly in a bag fitted with a fine plain nozzle. Cut cake in half.

Spread half the remaining cream on 1 piece of cake. Spoon pineapple on top. Place other piece of cake on top and spoon remaining cream on top. Pipe on shell border of jelly around top edge of cake. Pipe lines of red currant jelly in the center. Makes 6 servings.

## Christmas Mincemeat Tart

| | |
|---|---|
| 1¼ **cups all-purpose flour** | **Vegetable shortening** |
| ¼ **teaspoon salt** | 1 **(1-pound 12-ounce) jar** |
| ⅓ **cup vegetable oil** | **mincemeat** |
| 1 **to 2 tablespoons ice-cold** | 3 **tablespoons rum** |
| **water** | |

Combine flour, salt, and oil. Using pastry blender, work mixture until it forms particles the size of small peas. Add water, a tablespoon at a time, until mixture starts to form a ball. Using your hands, press mixture into flat disk. Place dough disk onto floured surface; roll into 8-inch circle, using 8-inch-round cake pan to form perfect circle.

Line bottom of 8-inch-round glass cake pan with waxed paper; grease sides with vegetable shortening. Pour mincemeat into cake pan, spreading evenly. Place pastry circle over mincemeat; microwave on high 15 minutes. Cool for 10 minutes. Invert pan onto flat serving platter; remove waxed paper.

Drizzle rum over surface of tart. Serve with whipped cream. Makes 8 servings.

## *Butterscotch Sauce*

| | | | |
|---|---|---|---|
| **1** | **cup brown sugar** | **½** | **cup heavy cream** |
| **3** | **tablespoons butter** | **1** | **teaspoon vanilla** |

Measure sugar, butter, and cream into a 4-cup glass measuring cup. Cook on high for 1 minute, then on roast for 30 seconds and defrost for 20 seconds. Stir; add vanilla. Makes 1 cup (enough ice-cream topping for 6 servings)

## *English Custard Sauce*

| | | | |
|---|---|---|---|
| **1¾** | **cups milk** | **3** | **egg yolks** |
| **¼** | **cup sugar** | **1** | **tablespoon cornstarch** |

Pour 1-1/2 cups of milk into a 4-cup glass measuring cup. Add sugar and microwave on high for 2 minutes.

Stir egg yolks, cornstarch, and remaining 1/4 cup of cold milk together. Add hot milk and sugar. Cook on high for 1 minute. Stir briskly with a wire whisk. This sauce goes well with Apple Brown Betty or poached fruit. Makes 2 cups.

## *Hot Fudge Sauce*

| | | | |
|---|---|---|---|
| **2** | **squares unsweetened baking chocolate** | **1** | **cup sugar** |
| **½** | **cup water** | **6** | **ounces semisweet chocolate pieces** |
| **2** | **tablespoons butter** | **¼** | **cup heavy cream** |
| **¼** | **cup white corn syrup** | | |

Place baking chocolate on a plate and microwave on high for 1 minute.
Transfer melted chocolate to a 4-cup glass measuring cup and add water, butter, corn syrup, and sugar. Cook on high for 2 minutes. Stir in the semisweet chocolate and cream. The semisweet chocolate will melt in the heat of the sauce. Makes 1-1/2 cups.

**Note:** Add 1/4 cup of dark rum to this sauce if you are serving it with poached or canned pears.

## Caramel Custard

| | |
|---|---|
| ¼ cup granulated sugar | ⅓ cup sugar |
| 3 eggs | 2 cups milk |
| 2 egg yolks | 1 teaspoon vanilla extract |

Place sugar in a 1-quart glass or ceramic casserole Microwave 5 minutes on high. Swirl sugar around the casserole after 2 minutes so that it will melt evenly to form a caramel. The bowl will become hot, so use oven mitts. Rotate casserole to coat the bottom and sides evenly with caramel.

Stir eggs, egg yolks, and sugar together until just combined. Heat milk in a 4-cup glass measuring cup for 2 minutes on high. Stir hot milk into eggs and sugar. Add vanilla and pour into caramel-lined casserole. Cook uncovered on low for 8 minutes. Stir custard and rotate the dish 1/4 of a turn every 2 minutes. Cool.

Chill custard for 4 hours and invert on a serving plate with a small rim. The caramel will form a sauce around the custard. Makes 6 servings.

## Chocolate Pudding

| | |
|---|---|
| 6 ounces sweet chocolate | 3 cups milk |
| ½ cup sugar | 3 eggs, lightly beaten |
| 2 tablespoons cornstarch | 1 teaspoon vanilla |

Break chocolate into squares and put on a plate. Microwave on high for 2 minutes.

Measure sugar, cornstarch, and milk into a 1-quart glass or ceramic bowl and cook for 2 minutes. Stir in melted chocolate and lightly beaten eggs with a wire whisk and cook on roast setting for 4 minutes. Add vanilla. Stir and chill for 4 hours before serving. Makes 6 servings.

*Jam Layers*

## EQUIVALENT MEASURES

dash = 2 or 3 drops
pinch = amount that can be held
        between ends of thumb &
        forefinger
1 tablespoon = 3 teaspoons
¼ cup = 4 tablespoons
⅓ cup = 5 tablespoons + 1 teaspoon
½ cup = 8 tablespoons
1 cup = 16 tablespoons
1 pint = 2 cups
1 quart = 4 cups
1 gallon = 4 quarts
1 peck = 8 quarts
1 bushel = 4 pecks
1 pound = 16 ounces

## KITCHEN METRIC

measurements you will encounter
most often in recipes are: centimeter
(cm), milliliter (ml), gram (g),
kilogram (kg)

*cup equivalents* (volume):

| | | |
|---|---|---|
| ¼ | cup | = 60 ml |
| ⅓ | cup | = 85 ml |
| ½ | cup | = 125 ml |
| ⅔ | cup | = 170 ml |
| ¾ | cup | = 180 ml |
| 1 | cup | = 250 ml |
| 1¼ | cups | = 310 ml |
| 1½ | cups | = 375 ml |
| 2 | cups | = 500 ml |
| 3 | cups | = 750 ml |
| 5 | cups | = 1250 ml |

*spoonful equivalents* (volume):

| | | |
|---|---|---|
| ⅛ | teaspoon | = .5 ml |
| ¼ | teaspoon | = 1.5 ml |
| ½ | teaspoon | = 3 ml |
| ¾ | teaspoon | = 4 ml |
| 1 | teaspoon | = 5 ml |
| 1 | tablespoon | = 15 ml |
| 2 | tablespoons | = 30 ml |
| 3 | tablespoons | = 45 ml |

*pan sizes* (linear & volume):

1 inch = 2.5 cm
8-inch square = 20-cm square
9 × 13 × 1½-inch = 20 × 33 × 4-cm
10 × 6 × 2-inch = 25 × 15 × 5-cm
13 × 9 × 2-inch = 33 × 23 × 5-cm
7½ × 12 × 1½-inch = 18 × 30 × 4-cm
 (above are baking dishes, pans)
9 × 5 × 3-inch = 23 × 13 × 8-cm
 (loaf pan)
10-inch = 25 cm   12-inch = 30-cm
 (skillets)
1-quart = 1-liter   2-quart = 2-liter
 (baking dishes, by volume)
5- to 6-cup = 1.5-liter
 (ring mold)

*weight* (meat amounts;
 can & package sizes):

| | | |
|---|---|---|
| 1 | ounce | = 28 g |
| ½ | pound | = 225 g |
| ¾ | pound | = 340 g |
| 1 | pound | = 450 g |
| 1½ | pounds | = 675 g |
| 2 | pounds | = 900 g |
| 3 | pounds | = 1.4 kg (in recipes, amounts of meat above 2 pounds will generally be stated in kilograms) |
| 10 | ounces | = 280 g (most frozen vegetables) |
| 10½ | ounces | = 294 g (most condensed soups) |
| 15 | ounces | = 425 g (common can size) |
| 16 | ounces | = 450 g (common can size) |
| 1 | pound, 24 ounces | = 850 g (can size) |

## OVEN TEMPERATURES

275°F = 135°C
300°F = 149°C
325°F = 165°C
350°F = 175°C
375°F = 190°C
400°F = 205°C
425°F = 218°C
450°F = 230°C
500°F = 260°C

**Note** that Celsius temperatures are
sometimes rounded off to the nearest
reading ending in 0 or 5; the Celsius
thermometer is the same as
Centigrade, a term no longer used.